The Strange Case of

Dr Jekyll and Mr Hyde

Robert Louis Stevenson

Notes by Tony Burke

Longman
York Press

YORK PRESS
322 Old Brompton Road, London SW5 9JH

ADDISON WESLEY LONGMAN LIMITED
Edinburgh Gate, Harlow,
Essex CM20 2JE, United Kingdom
Associated companies, branches and representatives throughout the world

First published 1998

ISBN 0–582–36826–X

Designed by Vicki Pacey, Trojan Horse, London
Illustrations by Chris Price
Phototypeset by Gem Graphics, Trenance, Mawgan Porth, Cornwall
Colour reproduction and film output by Spectrum Colour
Produced by Addison Wesley Longman China Limited, Hong Kong

CONTENTS

PREFACE

York Notes are designed to give you a broader perspective on works of literature studied at GCSE and equivalent levels. We have carried out extensive research into the needs of the modern literature student prior to publishing this new edition. Our research showed that no existing series fully met students' requirements. Rather than present a single authoritative approach, we have provided alternative viewpoints, empowering students to reach their own interpretations of the text. York Notes provide a close examination of the work and include biographical and historical background, summaries, glossaries, analyses of characters, themes, structure and language, cultural connections and literary terms.

If you look at the Contents page you will see the structure for the series. However, there's no need to read from the beginning to the end as you would with a novel, play, poem or short story. Use the Notes in the way that suits you. Our aim is to help you with your understanding of the work, not to dictate how you should learn.

York Notes are written by English teachers and examiners, with an expert knowledge of the subject. They show you how to succeed in coursework and examination assignments, guiding you through the text and offering practical advice. Questions and comments will extend, test and reinforce your knowledge. Attractive colour design and illustrations improve clarity and understanding, making these Notes easy to use and handy for quick reference.

York Notes are ideal for:

- Essay writing
- Exam preparation
- Class discussion

The author of these Notes, Tony Burke, is Head of English in a large comprehensive school in Swindon, Wiltshire. He has contributed to issues concerning English and Education in a number of radio programmes, is a senior examiner for the NEAB and has been involved in assessment work in English at Key Stage Three for a national consortium.

The text used in these Notes is the Penguin Popular Classics edition (1994).

Health Warning: **This study guide will enhance your understanding, but should not replace the reading of the original text and/or study in class.**

INTRODUCTION

HOW TO STUDY A NOVEL

You have bought this book because you wanted to study a novel on your own. This may supplement classwork.

- You will need to read the novel several times. Start by reading it quickly for pleasure, then read it slowly and carefully. Further readings will generate new ideas and help you to memorise the details of the story.
- Make careful notes on themes, plot and characters of the novel. The plot will change some of the characters. Who changes?
- The novel may not present events chronologically. Does the novel you are reading begin at the beginning of the story or does it contain flashbacks and a muddled time sequence? Can you think why?
- How is the story told? Is it narrated by one of the characters or by an all-seeing ('omniscient') narrator?
- Does the same person tell the story all the way through? Or do we see the events through the minds and feelings of a number of different people.
- Which characters does the narrator like? Which characters do you like or dislike? Do your sympathies change during the course of the book? Why? When?
- Any piece of writing (including your notes and essays) is the result of thousands of choices. No book had to be written in just one way: the author could have chosen other words, other phrases, other characters, other events. How could the author of your novel have written the story differently? If events were recounted by a minor character how would this change the novel?

Studying on your own requires self-discipline and a carefully thought-out work plan in order to be effective. Good luck.

ROBERT LOUIS STEVENSON'S BACKGROUND

Childhood

Robert Louis Stevenson was born in Edinburgh in 1850, the son of Thomas Stevenson, an engineer who, like his ancestors, built many of the deep-sea lighthouses on the coasts of Scotland. His mother, Isabella Mary Balfour, came from a family containing members of the legal profession and ministers of the Church. It is not surprising, therefore, that Robert Louis's childhood was shaped by the strict code of respectability of the Victorian middle class in Edinburgh.

Ill health

He suffered numerous health problems in childhood, chiefly due to an affection of the lungs, a condition which was to plague him throughout his life. His father was often absent on business and his mother herself suffered from an illness of the lungs, rendering her unable to care for her son. This task was given to his nurse, Alison Cunningham or 'Cummy', a fundamentalist Christian, with whom he developed his closest relationship.

Early influence

In fact, Robert Louis spent most of his early years in his bedroom where Cummy would labour to teach him the difference between the pursuit of a life of good or evil, the latter course leading, inevitably, to the everlasting torments of Hell. She made sure that Robert Louis was not spared the details of these torments, causing him to suffer terrifying nightmares, which he often recalled in his memoirs and which afflicted him throughout his life. He also recalled that she would try to convince him that 'there are but two camps in the world – one of the perfectly pious and respectable, one of the perfectly profane, mundane and vicious; one mostly on its knees and singing hymns, the other on the high road to the gallows and the bottomless pit.'

It was from one of his adult nightmares that *The Strange Case of Dr Jekyll and Mr Hyde* grew, a story which was to refute Cummy's simplistic doctrine, and argue that there is light and dark in all mankind. In the words of Jekyll, 'man is not truly one, but truly two'.

The two faces of Edinburgh

Stevenson grew up in an Edinburgh which itself had two faces: the prosperous, middle-class New Town, where he himself lived, and the 'old black city' with its poverty, disease and overcrowding. This was also a city with a macabre past, which fed the young man's developing imagination and taste for horror and the supernatural. Stories of William 'Deacon' Brodie, well respected craftsman by day, criminal by night and hanged in 1788, and also of Burke and Hare, the 'body snatchers', were well remembered in the city and, indeed, in his childhood bedroom Stevenson possessed a cabinet made by Brodie.

Stevenson's own double life

When he was seventeen and studying engineering at Edinburgh University, Robert Louis would spend a great deal of time at night in the Old Town. It has been argued that he himself, like Jekyll, was leading a double life, respectable by day, debauched by night but, although he enjoyed a bohemian lifestyle with his fellow students, his witnessing of these double standards amongst the middle classes made him determined to avoid hypocrisy and to react against the strict Scottish Presbyterian background which he felt helped to create it.

Adulthood

Stevenson left Edinburgh in 1873. On one of his many journeys abroad, he met and married his American wife Fanny Osbourne. They settled in Bournemouth in 1884. By this time, Stevenson had achieved fame with the publication of *Treasure Island* in 1883, but his serious health problems persisted and he hoped that the milder climate would help his congested lungs. Although the period between 1884 and 1887 saw a sharp decline in his health, when there were frequent bouts of haemorrhaging (his 'Bluidy Jack' as he called it), he was to publish *A Child's Garden of Verses, More Arabian Nights* and *Prince Otto* (1885); *The Strange Case of Dr Jekyll and Mr Hyde* and *Kidnapped* (1886); and *The Merry Men* and *Underwoods* (1887).

The South Seas

In 1887 he left England for the South Seas and made his home on Samoa for the rest of his life. Other significant works include *The Black Arrow* (1888) and the unfinished masterpiece *Weir of Hermiston* (1896). Works which are, perhaps, more directly connected with the subject matter explored in *Jekyll and Hyde* include *The Master of Ballantrae* (1889); the 'Tale of Tod Lapraik' in *Catriona* (1893); the play *Deacon Brodie, or, The Double Life* (1878) and the short stories 'The Body Snatcher' (1884), 'Markheim' and 'Olalla'. Other contemporary writers explored the **theme** (see Literary Terms) of man's double nature. Perhaps the most notable of these are Edgar Allan Poe in his short stories 'William Wilson' and 'The Tell Tale Heart', Mary Shelley in *Frankenstein*, Oscar Wilde in *The Picture of Dorian Gray* (1891) and Dostoevsky in *Crime and Punishment* and the short story 'The Double' (1846). In Scotland, James Hogg's *Confessions of a Justified Sinner* (1824) may well have had a profound impact on Stevenson.

CONTEXT & SETTING

The beast in man

Robert Louis Stevenson wrote this novel during his period in Bournemouth, 1884–7. The **setting** (see Literary Terms) appears to be Victorian London yet, as many have noted, he clearly has Edinburgh in mind with, like Jekyll, its twin identities, the prosperous and respectable New Town and the Old Town of poverty and desperation. Much of the novel takes place with the city at night as a backcloth. The characters always seem to be coming and going either late at night or in the early hours of the morning. The meagre light comes from the many flickering street lamps which swing in the wind and the pale moon which is often hidden by low cloud and fog.

The theme of 'the double'

Dr Jekyll and Mr Hyde was not the only story which expressed Stevenson's fascination with the dual personality of man. In two other works, the short story 'Markheim' and the play *Deacon Brodie* there are characters who also lead double lives. In 1859 Charles Darwin, in *On the Origin of Species,* had thrust into the Victorian consciousness his unpalatable theory that mankind was, in fact, descended from apes. Stevenson would have been well aware of the controversy which grew from these ideas and sought a vehicle on which to launch his ideas about 'the beast in man' and the attempt to hide, if not to subdue, animal passions. In Stevenson's words *Dr Jekyll and Mr Hyde* is about 'that damned old business of the war in the members' and because of the strictures of religion and conventional morality, men were forced to hide their secret desires in their public lives and indulge them at night in the darker, seedier parts of the city.

Repressed sexual desires

Those who were especially prey to these animal passions were men who believed that they could exist perfectly well 'without the aid of women', men like the characters in Stevenson's novel – Enfield (where exactly had he been to come home 'about three o'clock of a black winter morning'?), Utterson, Lanyon and Jekyll. There are repeated references to locked doors and cabinets and secret chambers reinforcing the idea that the beast must not only be hidden but imprisoned. It is clear that *Dr Jekyll and Mr Hyde* is, at least partly, about sexual repression, although the subject of sex itself is never explicitly mentioned in the text.

Contemporary psychology

Interestingly, at the same time as Stevenson was writing his novel, the French neurologist Charcot was using hypnosis as a means of revealing hidden aspects of the human personality. One of his public displays was witnessed by Sigmund Freud whose *Interpretation of Dreams*, to be published in 1901, argued that dreams were an expression of repressed sexual desires. Published in 1886 Krafft-Ebing's *Psychopathia Sexualis* attempted to analyse the war between man's basic, beastlike instincts and the need to conform to conventional moral standards and presented a series of case studies of sexual perversion. Although Stevenson may not have read this study, it does serve to illustrate some of the intellectual and psychological concerns of the time. The fact that he presents part of his novel as a casebook provides another link with contemporary thinking.

'The Beast of Whitechapel'

It is interesting to note that the notorious 'Jack the Ripper' crimes, in which five prostitutes were brutally murdered and mutilated in Whitechapel in the East End of London, took place within two years of the publication of Stevenson's novel and at the same time as a dramatised version was running in the West End.

Art mirrors life

At the time, these events and *Dr Jekyll and Mr Hyde* became confused in the public consciousness. People were not really sure which had come first and some of those who did know accused Stevenson of putting ideas in the murderer's mind. One journalist writing at the time concluded that, 'There seems to be a tolerably realistic impersonation of Mr Hyde at large in Whitechapel'. What the murders did reveal, however, was the kind of world that Stevenson was well aware of in the Old Town of his native Edinburgh, a world of poverty and despair where the rich and powerful would prey on the weak and defenceless.

CHRONOLOGY

Literary context	Year	Life of Stevenson
1818 Mary Shelley's *Frankenstein*	1818	
1824 James Hogg's *Confessions of a Justified Sinner*	1824	
	1850	Robert Louis Stevenson born in Edinburgh
1859 Darwin's *On the Origin of Species*	1859	
	1862-3	Enters Edinburgh University to study engineering. Travels with parents to the Riviera and Germany
	1871	Abandons engineering and studies law
	1872	Passes preliminary exam for the Scottish bar
	1873	Serious quarrels with father over his religion and morals. After this and ill health goes to Suffolk to stay with cousins, the Balfours. Meets Frances Sitwell, who will become a great influence. After further ill health travels to the South of France
	1874	Returns to Edinburgh. Contributes to the *Cornhill Magazine*
	1875	Called to the Scottish Bar but does not practise as a barrister
	1876	Makes a canoe trip in northern France. Meets an American, Fanny Osbourne, who is married with two children
	1878	Fanny returns to her husband in America but begins divorce proceedings. Publishes *Edinburgh: Picturesque Notes and an Inland Voyage*
	1879	Spends time in France, Scotland and London. Bouts of severe illness. Joins Fanny in America. Publishes *Travels with a Donkey*

World events	Year	Stevenson's life
	1880	Marries Fanny in San Francisco. Later they return to Scotland. Writes *Deacon Brodie*, his first play, in collaboration with W.E. Henley, reveals a central character with a double personality, anticipating *Jekyll and Hyde*
	1881	Writes *Treasure Island* and begins *The Travelling Companion* which forecasts *Jekyll and Hyde.* Dissatisfied with this work, he destroys it
	1882	Moves to France. Publishes *New Arabian Nights*
	1883	Publishes *Treasure Island*
	1884	Seriously ill, returns to Bournemouth, his home until 1887. Publishes short story *The Body Snatcher*
1885 French neurologist Charcot gives public display of hypnotism in Paris	1885	Publishes *A Child's Garden of Verses* and writes *Dr Jekyll and Mr Hyde*
1886 Krafft-Ebing's *Psychopathia Sexualis*	1886	Publishes *Dr Jekyll and Mr Hyde* and *Kidnapped*
	1887	Death of Thomas Stevenson. Robert Louis sails to America
1888 The 'Jack the Ripper' murders take place in the East End	1888	Visits the South Pacific. Sullivan's dramatised version of *Dr Jekyll and Mr Hyde* put on in London's West End
	1889	Begins life in Samoa. Publishes T*he Master of Ballantrae*
	1890	Because of serious ill health decides never to return to Britain
1891 Oscar Wilde's *Dorian Gray*	1891	
	1894	After working for long hours on *Weir of Hermiston*, dies of a cerebral haemorrhage
1901 Freud's *Interpretation of Dreams*	1901	

SUMMARIES

GENERAL SUMMARY

Section I (The mystery of Mr Hyde)

The story of the door

Search for Mr Hyde

Dr Jekyll quite at ease

Dr Henry Jekyll is a well-respected physician and chemist. Gabriel Utterson, his friend and lawyer, is concerned about his relationship with a mysterious Mr Hyde to whom Jekyll has left a quarter of a million pounds in a Will which he has placed under Utterson's guardianship. Although he has serious misgivings about this arrangement and suspects blackmail, Utterson agrees to administer it whatever the circumstances. Dr Hastie Lanyon, another friend and fellow scientist, has long been deeply suspicious about some of the experiments which Jekyll has been carrying out in his laboratory and has become distanced from him. Utterson's cousin, Richard Enfield, tells the lawyer that he had witnessed Hyde colliding with and then trampling over an eight-year-old girl near the squalid rear entrance to Jekyll's laboratory and that when ordered to pay some compensation, drew the money from Jekyll's account. Enfield is particularly struck, as are all who witnessed the deed, by the feelings of repugnance and loathing which Hyde inspires in him.

Section II (The terror begins)

The Carew murder case

Incident of the letter

Later, in another part of the city, Hyde, witnessed by a maidservant who recognises him, brutally murders the elderly Sir Danvers Carew, MP, who is delivering a letter to Utterson. The police are called and they search Hyde's rooms, finding evidence of a hurried exit. Amongst other things, they discover the remains of the murder weapon and some burnt papers, including what is left of a cheque book. Later, Utterson is able to compare examples of Hyde's and Jekyll's handwriting and notices their remarkable similarity. After the seeming disappearance of Hyde, Jekyll once more becomes a public figure much concerned with good deeds.

Section III (The beast in man)

Remarkable incident of Dr Lanyon

Incident at the window

Some time later, Lanyon, having had a shock which has seriously damaged his health, hands Utterson a sealed package. He stresses that this must not be opened until after Jekyll's death but he refuses to discuss its contents. Lanyon says that he wants no more to do with his former friend Jekyll and, soon after, dies. Jekyll once more retires into seclusion, refusing to see any of his friends. While walking past Jekyll's house, Utterson and Enfield catch sight of him at his window and although he seems pleased to see them his face suddenly changes to an expression of terror and despair and he quickly disappears from view.

The last night

Jekyll's manservant Poole urgently calls on Utterson for help, believing that his master has been murdered and that the person who has locked himself away is Hyde. Utterson breaks into the laboratory and finds that Hyde has poisoned himself and is dying. Although an extensive search is carried out, there is no trace of Jekyll.

Section IV (The revelation)

Dr Lanyon's narrative

'Dr Lanyon's Narrative' tells of how Jekyll had begged him to go to his laboratory where he should collect some specific drugs. Lanyon was to give these to a messenger who would arrive at his house at midnight. The strange messenger arrives. It is obviously Hyde. He mixes the potion and while Lanyon watches, transforms himself into Jekyll.

Section V (Struggle and fall)

Henry Jekyll's full statement of the case

This section describes his weariness of the struggle between the public, respectable side of his life and its opposite, the dark, secretive and dishonourable. In it, he gives the details of his research into the separation of the good and evil sides of his personality and the discovery of the potion which enabled him to do this.

At first, he has only to drink the potion to transform himself into either Jekyll or Hyde and the good in him is clearly in control but the evil side gradually begins to gain in strength until one day he transforms into Hyde involuntarily. Realising that he has run out of the drugs which he needs in increased dosage to subdue Hyde, Jekyll begins a desperate but unsuccessful search for them. He realises that Hyde is now in almost complete control and contemplates suicide.

DETAILED SUMMARIES

SECTION I THE MYSTERY OF MR HYDE

STORY OF THE DOOR

Notice the many contradictions in Utterson's character.

The first chapter introduces us to one of the two main characters in the novel, Gabriel Utterson. Two long paragraphs are devoted to a description of this complex character who is 'cold, scanty and embarrassed in discourse; backward in sentiment; lean, long, dusty, dreary, and yet somehow lovable' (p. 9) (see Characters). Utterson is with his relation Mr Richard Enfield ('the well-known man about town') in a 'busy quarter of London', who draws his attention to a door which stands out in contrast to the rest of the buildings in the street because of its shabby and dilapidated state.

We first hear of Edward Hyde.

Enfield then begins to tell Utterson 'a very odd story' about an incident which he had been involved in while returning home through this area at a very late hour. Enfield had witnessed an accidental collision between a man walking quickly and a young girl running, which took place at the corner of a street. There was nothing unusual about this but the man's reaction was, in

Enfield's words, 'hellish to see', for he 'trampled calmly' over the body of the girl, leaving her screaming in pain and terror. Enfield chased and caught the culprit, bringing him back to the scene of the crime where the child's family and a doctor had gathered about her. The man appeared to be calm in the presence of his accusers yet he inspired loathing and hatred in all those around him. When threatened with a public scandal, the man agreed with apparent coolness to compensate the child with £100 for the child's family. To Enfield' surprise, he then produced a key and opened the very door which had prompted Enfield to tell his strange story to Utterson. He returned with some cash and a cheque signed by another gentleman well known to Enfield, who does not reveal the name to Utterson at that point. Naturally, the bank is not open at that early hour of the morning, so the doctor, the girl's father and Enfield accompanied the man to Enfield's chambers where they remained until the morning, when, to general surprise, the cheque was found to be genuine.

Notice the peculiar effect which the strange man has on all those who encountered him.

Enfield naturally suspects blackmail. He returns once more in his conversation to the subject of the odd house with the singular door which it seems is only visited by the strange man of Enfield's story who, he had found, lived elsewhere 'in some square or other' in Soho. Although he had made such an unpleasant impression on Enfield he finds it difficult to describe him to Utterson and when he reveals the name of this man as Hyde, Utterson's suspicions are confirmed. He knows full well whose account the money was drawn from and whose laboratories the door leads to. However, he does not reveal this knowledge to Enfield and both men agree to keep what they have been discussing very much to themselves.

Dr Jekyll's house and laboratory

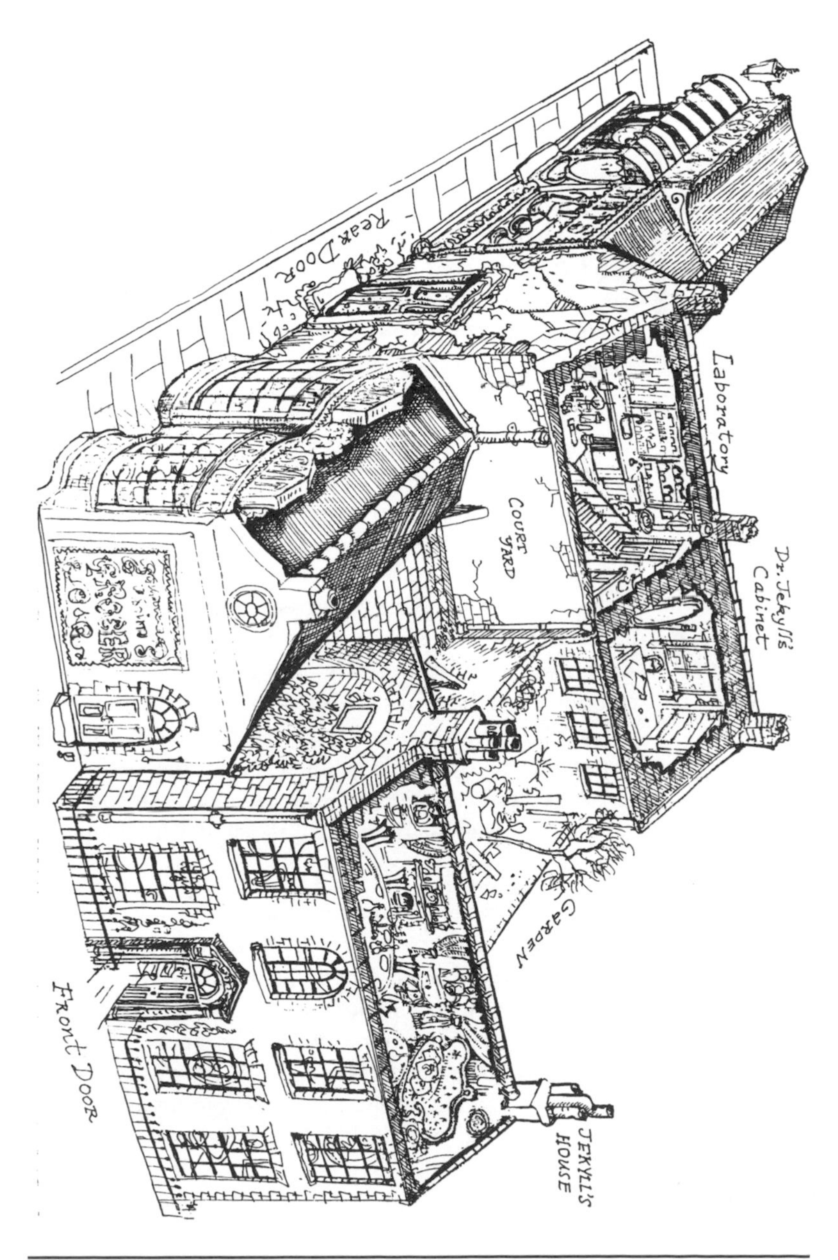

COMMENT

This chapter introduces us to the major **theme** (see Literary Terms & Themes) of the novel, of the duality of nature – that often things are not what they seem. The description of Utterson reveals several contradictions in his character (see Characters) and the neglected, dingy appearance of the door strikes an incongruous note in the otherwise smart and pleasant street. The incident involving Hyde is set in the early part of the morning in the almost deserted lamp-lit streets, a **setting** (see Literary Terms) which is used throughout the novel.

Try to build up a mental picture of Hyde.

Enfield's first impression of Hyde reveals other contradictions. He is 'cool' yet underneath 'frightened', and although there is nothing particularly displeasing about him physically, he provokes intense feelings of hatred within all around him. We see here how Hyde begins to bring out the worst in people. Enfield, looking at the angry crowd surrounding Hyde, declares that he 'never saw a circle of such hateful faces'. Even the doctor, an ordinary man 'and about as emotional as a bagpipe' is roused to murderous intent. When Hyde draws the cheque from the account of a respectable gentleman, blackmail is immediately suspected, and it is automatically assumed that this gentleman has some disgraceful secret which he must conceal.

Note the importance of secrecy.

We become aware of the atmosphere of secrecy within this society and that a reluctance to ask questions is a commonly held golden rule. Everyone, it seems, has something to hide. The **setting** contributes to this **atmosphere** (see Literary Terms). The strange door which Enfield remarks upon is always locked, the windows in the rest of the house always shut and the buildings around the 'court' huddled together as if in conspiracy.

GLOSSARY

Cain's heresy refers to Genesis 4 in which Cain murders his brother Abel

Juggernaut from the Hindi, meaning 'lord of the world', an idol of which was dragged on an enormous car under which devotees would throw themselves to be crushed

gave a view halloa (hunting term) gave a cry to urge the hounds, when the fox was sighted

harpies (Greek mythology) half-woman and half-bird creatures which attacked humans

the very pink of the proprieties upright to the highest degree

Queer Street an imaginary street where people in trouble, financial or otherwise, are supposed to live

SEARCH FOR MR HYDE

Consider the precise wording of Jekyll's Will.

Utterson returns home that evening to study the contents of the Will of his friend, Dr Henry Jekyll. Although he is in charge of it, he refused to have anything to do with its making and he is deeply troubled as to its contents. In the Will, Jekyll states that, in the case of his death, all his possessions should pass to his 'friend and benefactor Edward Hyde', and also that should the doctor disappear or be inexplicably absent for three months or more, Hyde should take up his position at once. Previously, Utterson, ignorant of Hyde, had thought of this document as an act of madness, but now that part of the sinister nature of Hyde has been revealed to him, he, like Enfield, believes that Hyde has some hold over Jekyll, who is trying to conceal some disgrace.

We first hear of Jekyll's strange experiments.

Utterson decides to visit the eminent Dr Lanyon, friend and colleague to both men, whom he hopes may be able to shed some light on this disturbing matter. Lanyon reveals that he has seen little of Jekyll recently and that their professional relationship as fellow scientists ended more than ten years ago when Jekyll's ideas and experiments became 'too fanciful' for him. This is the first indication that Jekyll has been dabbling in unconventional science and, although this has clearly disturbed Lanyon, Utterson is relieved that it is only a disagreement over scientific matters. Lanyon declares that he knows nothing at all of Hyde.

The rational Utterson has a terrible nightmare.

That night, Utterson has a dream in which the terrible scene of Hyde trampling over the child is re-enacted and also he sees a vision of his friend Jekyll under the power of some terrifying faceless figure. He awakes determined to see the face of Mr Hyde and decides to pursue him.

We first meet Edward Hyde.

After several unsuccessful attempts, Utterson intercepts Hyde as he is about to enter the strange door mentioned earlier by Enfield. At first, Hyde deliberately avoids looking directly at the lawyer but Utterson asks to see his face so that he will know him in future. Hyde not only does so, but gives him his Soho address. The lawyer's suspicions are immediately aroused; he is convinced that Hyde is preparing to take advantage of Jekyll's Will. When Hyde asks Utterson how he came to know him, the lawyer says that Jekyll had told him. At this, Hyde laughs angrily, apparently knowing that Utterson is lying, before disappearing 'with extraordinary quickness' through the door.

Utterson reflects upon the singular appearance of Hyde, yet still cannot understand why he is filled with so much 'unknown disgust, loathing and fear' in his presence.

Utterson is convinced of blackmail.

The lawyer decides to visit Jekyll at his home and is admitted by Poole, the elderly servant who explains that his master is out. When questioned, Poole reveals that all the servants have orders to obey Hyde and that they see little of him in the house because he spends most of his time in the laboratory, using the 'old dissecting-room door' for entry and exit. Utterson leaves, full of sorrow for Jekyll who, he is convinced, is being haunted by the re-emergence of a past crime, which Hyde is using to blackmail him.

Even Utterson has something to hide.

The lawyer thinks about his own life which, although largely blameless, contains some guilty secrets which could be used against him and that, if such 'respectable' men have things to hide, what would the villainous Hyde be at pains to conceal? He decides to pursue Hyde to discover his secret and thwart his attempts to inherit from Jekyll's Will.

COMMENT

We are introduced to the strange contents of Jekyll's Will and, like Utterson, forced to conclude that Jekyll is the victim of blackmail. Notice again the atmosphere of secrecy as the lawyer collects the Will from 'the most private part' of the safe within his business room.

We first meet Dr Hastie Lanyon.

When we are introduced to Lanyon, once again the dual nature of the personality is hinted at when his effusive welcome of Utterson is described as being 'somewhat theatrical to the eye'. Clearly, his dispute with Jekyll centres around the latter's unscientific work and we are left to speculate as to its nature. What kind of work must Jekyll be involved in to cause so much offence to his old friend that he loses his temper in Utterson's presence when referring to it?

Utterson's dream once again draws on the **theme** (see Literary Terms & Themes) of secrecy. He lies in his 'curtained room' in 'the gross darkness of the night' and again the **setting** (see Literary Terms) is the city at night with 'a great field of lamps'. The mysterious figure he sees in these dreams has no face for him to recognise and it moves quickly and 'stealthily' through the houses and labyrinths of the city as if determined to avoid detection.

When Utterson conceals himself while waiting to surprise Hyde, the description of the quietness of the nocturnal city in which the slightest sounds are amplified heightens the tension and sharpens our anticipation of the arrival of Hyde. Hyde's 'hissing intake of breath' strengthens the beastlike impression of the man whose momentary fear is rapidly replaced by his customary coolness. We are given the first clear impression of Hyde as Utterson attempts to explain why he was filled with such loathing at the sight of him. Once again the contradictions appear as Hyde's 'murderous mixture of timidity and boldness' are noted and the inhuman qualities of the man are strengthened with Utterson's description of him as 'troglodytic'.

Note the contrast between Hyde's style of speech and that of Utterson.

The chapter ends with the lawyer in extremely low spirits. Clearly Hyde has had a profound impact upon him, causing him to feel 'a nausea and distaste of life'. He somehow feels forced to confront the fact that he too has been responsible for certain wrongs in his life, which he has taken great care to hide. What is it within their own lives which might cause them to feel the same?

Why does Hyde seem to have this effect on Utterson?

GLOSSARY

volume of some dry divinity a dull book about religion
holograph a document written entirely in the handwriting of the person whose signature it carries
M.D., D.C.L., LL.D., F.R.S. Doctor of Medicine, Doctor of Civil Law, Doctor of Laws, Fellow of the Royal Society
Damon and Pythias (Greek mythology) two inseparable friends. When Pythias was sentenced to death by Dionysius, Damon offered to take his place. Neither wanted to live if it meant that the other perished
troglodytic primitive, cave dwelling
Dr Fell an unpleasant person who causes feelings of dislike which are difficult to give any obvious reason for

statute of limitations a law protecting a person from prosecution after a period of time has elapsed
pede claudo walking hesitantly

DR JEKYLL WAS QUITE AT EASE

We first meet Henry Jekyll.

Two weeks later, Jekyll invites some of his old friends to dinner. Utterson remains behind when they have gone to discuss the Will, once again expressing his strong disapproval. Jekyll is cheerful and confident when seeking to reassure his friend but when the lawyer tries to talk of Hyde and what terrible things he has learned of him, the doctor grows pale and refuses to be drawn on this subject. Although he had earlier dismissed his other friend, Lanyon, as an 'ignorant, blatant pedant', Jekyll declares his respect and admiration for Utterson, telling him that things are not so bad as he thinks and that he could rid himself of Hyde whenever he chooses. He does, however, not only beg Utterson to keep these matters very much to himself but also to make sure that Hyde receives what is legally due to him should anything happen to Jekyll.

Think why Jekyll is so hostile to Lanyon.

COMMENT

It is in this chapter that we first meet Henry Jekyll. Bearing in mind the **atmosphere** (see Literary Terms) of secrecy which pervades the novel, notice that his face is described as having 'a slyish cast'. Also, he particularly values Utterson in preference to his other friends – 'the light-hearted and loose-tongued'. What things can you find out about Utterson's character in this and earlier chapters which lead others within his social circle to hold the 'dry' lawyer in such particularly high regard? Jekyll's dismissal of Lanyon is presumed by Utterson to be based on an argument over scientific matters. Look again at the description of Lanyon (pp. 18–19). What other reasons might Jekyll have for

Think about what this hints at in Jekyll's character.

his hostile attitude towards him? Jekyll is obviously deeply affected by Utterson's mention of Hyde as the lawyer tries to get him to reveal his reasons for the bizarre arrangements in his Will. Notice once again how the doctor convinces Utterson of the need for absolute secrecy in the matter.

GLOSSARY

hide-bound pedant narrow minded and conventional in thinking

TEST YOURSELF (Section I: Chapters 1–3)

A *Identify the speaker.*

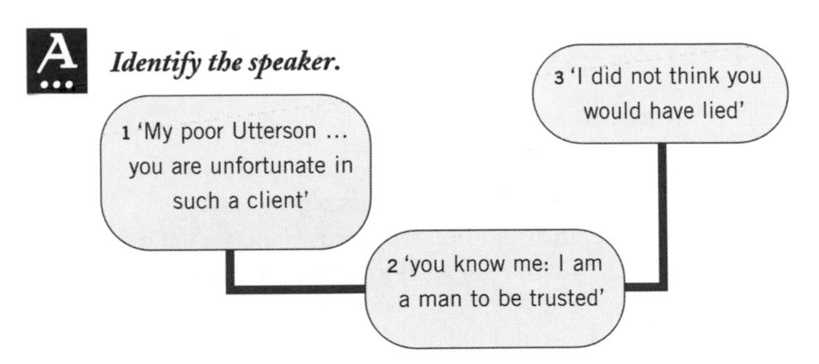

Identify the person 'to whom' this comment refers.

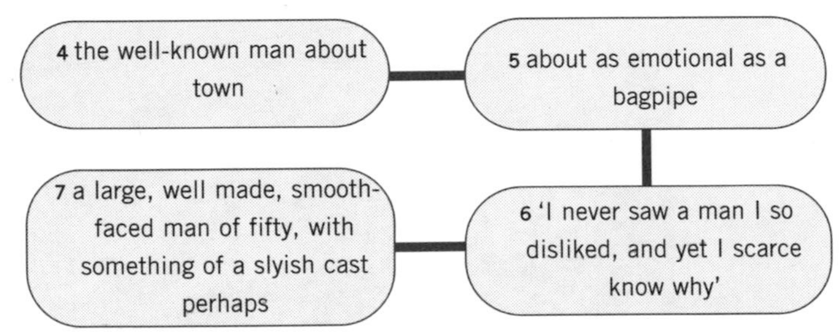

Check your answers on page 80.

B *Consider these issues.*

a The detailed description of the contradictions in Utterson's character.

b The author's purpose in contrasting the appearance of the door with the rest of the street.

c The effect of Hyde on the rest of the characters.

d How the author reveals the dual nature of Jekyll's personality.

e The author's use of the mask **motif** (see Literary Terms).

f The development of the **theme** (see Literary Terms) of secrecy.

g How the author arouses our fears for Jekyll through the reading of the Will.

h How the author heightens the drama and tension through the description of Utterson's dream.

i The author's creation of **atmosphere** (see Literary Terms) in the description of the nocturnal city.

j The style of language which the author gives to Hyde in contrast to that of Utterson.

SECTION II THE TERROR BEGINS

THE CAREW MURDER CASE

Contrast the description of Carew with that of Hyde.

London is shocked by the vicious murder of Sir Danvers Carew, MP, which is witnessed by a maidservant from her bedroom window. She describes how the victim, 'an aged and beautiful gentleman' whom she did not recognise and who seemed to have 'an innocent and old-world kindness of disposition' encountered a very small man whom she did know, Mr Hyde.

What has caused Hyde to react in this way?

Although the elderly man seemed to address Hyde with perfect politeness, Hyde, without replying, suddenly flew into a wild rage and began to batter the helpless man with his walking stick, causing him to fall to the ground. At this, Hyde began to trample on his victim with such force that the maid could clearly hear the shattering of the bones. When the police were called, they found the 'mangled' body of the victim and half of the murderer's walking stick. On searching the body they find all his possessions, including a sealed and stamped envelope addressed to Mr Utterson. The police contact the lawyer who identifies him as

Sir Danvers Carew, MP. Utterson recognises the broken walking stick as the remainder of that which he himself had given Jekyll many years ago and he takes the police to Hyde's house.

Utterson is given more evidence of blackmail.

When they arrive, they find that Hyde has fled, leaving evidence of his quick departure with clothes and possessions scattered about. The other half of the murder weapon is also found and in the fireplace are the remains of burned papers, including part of a cheque book. When the police check Hyde's account at the bank, they find him several thousand pounds in credit and decide to wait for him there. Utterson is less confident of Hyde's capture, knowing more of his mysterious and elusive past.

COMMENT

You will need to remind yourself of the ***themes*** *of the novel.*

The terrible incident in this chapter occurs almost a year after the end of the last chapter. What do you notice about the **setting** (see Literary Terms) for the murder of Sir Danvers? Although this resembles the **settings** for other incidents in the novel there is an important difference. What is that difference and how does it make the murder of major importance to the development of the **plot** (see Literary Terms)?

It is important to notice here that the maidservant gives a very precise description of Sir Danvers which contrasts sharply with that of Hyde. In fact it might be said that at this point the two men represent opposing sides of the human personality. Hyde here is in an uncontrollable fury. The 'innocent' old man with his 'well-founded self-content' seems to have provoked him into this state. How can a defenceless old man like this have caused such a dreadful outburst? The 'beast in man' (see Context & Setting) is clearly represented by Hyde here. Notice how his fury is described as 'ape-like'.

Note down other references to Hyde's beastlike qualities.

Look at the way Stevenson creates a feeling of horror without giving too many details.

This is certainly the most horrific passage in the book and Stevenson does not spare the reader the gruesome details. The victim's bones are 'audibly shattered', the body 'jumped upon the roadway', the body is 'mangled' and the murder weapon, a walking stick of 'very tough and heavy wood' is broken in half after being used to club the victim (p. 30). This would have been very shocking to the Victorian reader (see Context & Setting) and it certainly manages to disturb us too. We see here the author's taste for the macabre and horrific which he explores in some of his other works (see Robert Louis Stevenson's Background).

*Stevenson again explores the **theme** of hypocrisy.*

It is important to look at the behaviour of some of the minor characters in response to the murder. Once again, the contradictions in the human personality are explored. The shock of the police officer when the body is revealed as that of Sir Danvers is immediately supplanted by thoughts of 'professional ambition' (p. 31). His thoughts have obviously turned to what he can gain from this situation. The old woman at the rooms of Hyde 'had an evil face, smoothed by hypocrisy; but her manners were excellent' (p. 32). When she realises that the police want to speak to Hyde a 'flash of odious joy' (p. 32) appears upon her face. Although we can understand why she might want the terrible Mr Hyde to come to harm, we get the clear impression that she would generally delight in the misfortunes of others. What does this tell us about the author's view of human nature?

*Note the power of the **setting**.*

The **setting** (see Literary Terms) in this chapter is again very important. The fog once again contributes to the **atmosphere** (see Literary Terms) of gloom and secrecy and 'the dismal quarter of Soho' seems to Utterson 'like a district of some city in a nightmare'. The contrast between this area of the city and the luxury of Hyde's rooms within it once again points to the **theme** (see Literary Terms) of duality.

GLOSSARY

conflagration fire
gin palace public house for the consumption of alcoholic beverages
penny numbers goods which could be bought for a penny
slatternly slovenly, wretched
blackguardly evil looking

INCIDENT OF THE LETTER

There is a terrible change in Jekyll.

Utterson visits Jekyll, where he is admitted for the first time to his laboratory. He finds the doctor sickly and pale and asks him whether he has heard the news of the murder. Jekyll shudders at the mention of this topic and begs Utterson to believe him when he says that Hyde will never be heard of again. He shows the lawyer a letter written by Hyde, apparently delivered by hand, in which he apologises for the way he has repaid Jekyll's generosity, assuring him that he would certainly escape from London.

Jekyll a forger?

Before he leaves, Utterson asks Poole whether anything had been delivered by hand that day but the servant was sure that whatever had come to the house had only done so by post. Later, he shows the letter to his head clerk Mr Guest, who is something of a handwriting expert. When a dinner invitation arrives from Jekyll, Guest compares the two, finding the handwriting remarkably similar. Utterson is left convinced that Jekyll has forged the letter to protect Hyde.

COMMENT

The **atmosphere** (see Literary Terms) of secrecy continues in this chapter. Jekyll's laboratory is described **symbolically** (see Literary Terms) as a 'windowless structure' and the only three windows in the doctor's

Note down other ***symbols*** *of secrecy in the text.*

cabinet are barred with iron. The seemingly ever-present fog not only surrounds the building but even enters its interior, lying thickly. Notice that Jekyll looks 'deadly sick', his hand is 'cold' and he has a 'feverish manner' (p. 35). This is a marked contrast to the earlier chapter 'Doctor Jekyll is Quite at Ease' in which he appears as a 'large, well-made, smooth-faced man'.

Pay particular attention to the how the author's creates a brooding, sinister **atmosphere** (see Literary Terms) with the flickering light of the many street lamps and his **personification** (see Literary Terms) of the fog.

Utterson is a man whose very trade is the keeping of secrets.

The air of impending doom is reinforced with the description of the city as 'drowned'. The interior of the room contrasts with this as do the colours and flavours in the bottle of wine which Utterson had previously kept hidden in his cellar. His head clerk Mr Guest, we are told, shares some, but certainly not all, of his secrets. It is interesting that Guest is more perceptive than his master in recognising the similarity between the two types of handwriting. Why do you think this is? As in other chapters, a cloak of secrecy descends upon matters at the end. Guest is sworn to silence and the note is locked in Utterson' safe.

GLOSSARY

cupola a domed roof sometimes containing windows
cabinet private study
glass presses glass fronted cupboards
cheval-glass a mirror, set in a frame which can be tilted
carbuncles red precious stones

TEST YOURSELF (Section II: Chapters 4–5)

A *Identify the speaker.*

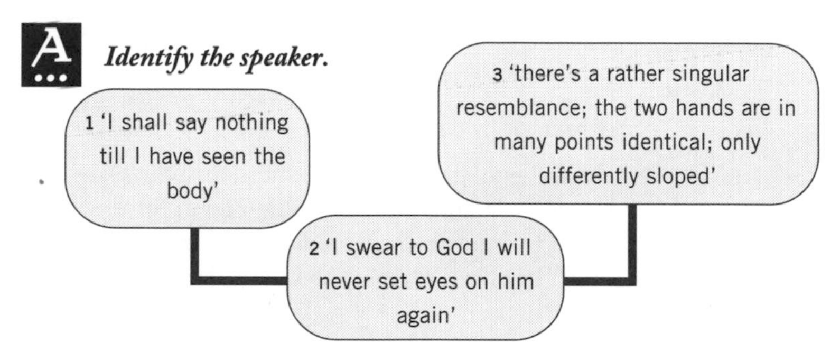

Identify the place to which this comment refers.

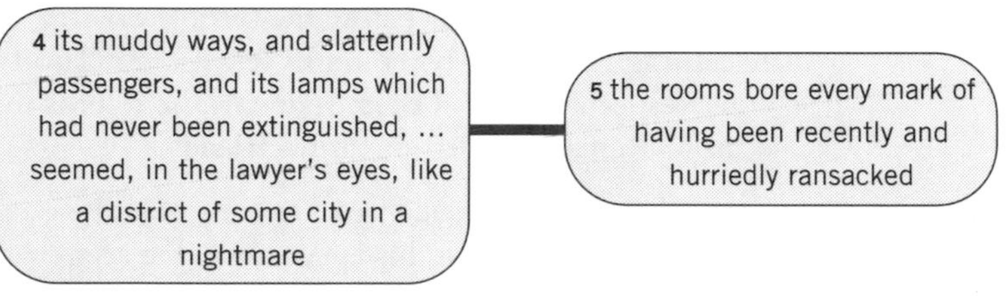

Check your answers on page 80.

B *Consider these issues.*

a The continued presence of the fog, again **personified** (see Literary Terms) by the author.

b The dramatic change in the appearance and emotions of Jekyll.

c The author's use of the handwriting expert to introduce a twist into the **plot** (see Literary Terms) and how he is made to seem more perceptive than Utterson.

d How we are led to share Utterson's theory of the reason for the 'forged' letter.

e The marked contrast in the descriptions of Hyde and Carew.

f How the author conveys the brutality and horror of the attack on Carew.

g The possible motive that Hyde could have for the attack.

h The author's use of precise descriptive detail of the city to create the sombre **atmosphere** (see Literary Terms).

i How the author reveals the duality of two of the minor characters.

j How the author reminds us of the effect Hyde has on all who meet him.

SECTION III THE BEAST IN MAN

REMARKABLE INCIDENT OF DR LANYON

His crimes are only hinted at here. Think about what Hyde might be capable of.

Despite the public outcry at the murder of Sir Danvers and the considerable rewards being offered for the capture of his murderer, Hyde has apparently vanished and much has been revealed about his dark secret past.

Utterson is hugely relieved, particularly as a remarkable change has come over his friend Jekyll, who has emerged much as he was before the terrible events concerning Hyde. For two months Jekyll is a pillar of public respectability, but then, suddenly, he returns to seclusion, refusing to see any of his friends.

There is a terrible change in Lanyon.

Alarmed at this, Utterson visits Dr Lanyon and is alarmed at the change in his appearance. He seems much older and frailer, this obviously due to some dreadful shock which he must have received. Lanyon is clearly a very frightened man and tells Utterson that he will surely meet his death very soon. When the lawyer asks him whether he has had any contact with Jekyll, Lanyon declares that he wants nothing more to do with his former friend and refuses even to talk about him. He apologises to Utterson for the seeming callousness of his attitude but assures him that he will learn of his reasons after his death.

Jekyll has become a recluse.

Utterson writes to Jekyll asking to see him and telling him of Lanyon's illness and hostility. Jekyll's reply is strangely written and full of misery. In it he says that he agrees with Lanyon, that he must never meet his friends again and begs Utterson to leave him alone for the sake of their friendship. Jekyll also writes of his terrible sufferings but stresses that he only has himself to blame.

Think why it is that Lanyon dies.

Three weeks later, Lanyon is dead and Utterson receives a package addressed to him in Lanyon's hand. Inside is a sealed envelope upon which is written 'not to be opened till the death or disappearance of Dr Henry Jekyll'. The word 'disappearance' has, for Utterson, disturbing echoes of Jekyll's Will and, from this moment, his desire to see his old friend begins to weaken. When he does visit, Poole tells him that Jekyll is very rarely seen, spending most of his time within the laboratory. Clearly the servant, conscious of the terrible silences and the complete change in habits, feels that his master's mind is deeply troubled.

COMMENT

Note that Jekyll has recovered as soon as Hyde disappears.

The remarkable disappearance of Hyde coincides with the equally remarkable upturn in the health and fortunes of Jekyll. Gone is the sickly figure living in seclusion because the evil influence which has tainted his life has removed himself. No longer the recluse, Jekyll throws himself into a very public life in which he embraces good. See if you can identify other examples in the text of characters who undergo a physical and emotional change for the worse.

Think about why these changes come about.

Almost as suddenly, the situation changes back again. Jekyll removes himself from society and we are presented once again with the **image** (see Literary Terms) of the locked door. Lanyon's altered appearance represents another dramatic change. Contrast Lanyon's description in the second chapter (p. 18) which is full of health and vitality with the new description of him (p. 41) in which he appears close to death.

At this point we are reminded of Lanyon's reference to his dispute with Jekyll (p. 19) and Jekyll's dismissal of him as 'an ignorant, blatant pedant' (p. 27).

Notice how Utterson recognises that Lanyon is a terrified man but that it is not his impending death which frightens him. He is firm when he admits that he is a doomed man but finds it hard to steady himself when Jekyll's name is mentioned. Clearly we are led to believe that Lanyon's altered state has something to do with his former colleague and friend and that Lanyon almost welcomes death. He says that 'if we knew all' we would all be glad to die. Think about what kind of knowledge he can be referring to; what he has learned to make him feel like this. If not death, consider what deep shock Lanyon has had to make him so frightened.

Utterson's letter to Jekyll provokes another unsatisfactory and miserable reply in which the doctor once again urges the need for closed doors, secrecy and silence. At the end of the chapter, Jekyll has withdrawn himself so much that even the servants in his household see very little of him.

GLOSSARY

ken knowledge
allusion to mention of
amities friendships
predecease to die before
mortify control, subdue

INCIDENT AT THE WINDOW

This is the chapter where Jekyll almost transforms into Hyde before Utterson and Enfield. We are not given details of what they actually see but we are left to feel that it must have been more than just a change of expression to provoke such horror.

Utterson is again walking with Enfield and they stop once more at the rear door to Jekyll's laboratory. They step into the courtyard because Utterson is still anxious to see his old friend and feels that if he can bring him out of his voluntary imprisonment he can do him some good. To his surprise, he sees Jekyll sitting disconsolately at one of the windows and when he asks about the doctor's health the latter replies that he is very low but that he will not have to go on suffering for much longer. Jekyll seems very pleased to see his old friend and he smilingly agrees to carry on the conversation, when suddenly his expression changes to one of 'abject terror and despair' before he slams the window shut. Although they only glimpse his face it is enough to frighten his two visitors who return home in almost complete silence 'with an answering horror in their eyes'.

COMMENT

Think about what is happening to Jekyll which was not happening before.

The most important incident in this brief chapter is the sudden change in the expression on Jekyll's smiling face to 'one of abject terror and despair'. This freezes the blood of Enfield and Utterson and the window is slammed shut. This incident shows that Jekyll is suffering from something which he cannot control and that the two men are deeply shocked at the transformation. We feel that it is not the expression on Jekyll's face which causes this shock but something much deeper seated which they recognise. Can it be the same recognition which hastened the death of Dr Lanyon?

GLOSSARY

whipping up the circulation exercising to make the blood course through the veins

THE LAST NIGHT

*Poole becomes one of the **narrators***

Utterson is at home one evening when he receives a visit from a terrified Poole. The servant suspects foul play and begs Utterson to return with him to Jekyll's laboratory. When they arrive, the servants are in a state of high anxiety. Poole takes him to the door of the doctor's cabinet, urging him to keep silent so that he can listen clearly and on no account to enter if invited to do so. These instructions unnerve the lawyer but he recovers himself and agrees to comply.

Poole announces Utterson's presence and a voice from within replies that he will not see him. The two men return to the house where the servant quizzes the lawyer on the nature of the voice which they have just heard. Utterson says that it is much changed but the servant is not satisfied with this judgement, declaring that it is not the voice of his master and that he should know, having lived with him for twenty years. Poole goes on to say that he is convinced that his master was murdered eight days previously when he heard him cry out in the name of God and that, since then, the only communication he has had with whoever or whatever is in the room has been in the form of desperate demands for a particular drug written on numerous sheets of paper. Poole added that despite the fact that he had tried various chemists, every time the drug was passed into the room it was later rejected as being impure.

Poole is convinced that Jekyll has been murdered by Hyde.

The servant then describes how he had seen the occupant of the room when he surprised him as he was searching for something but that what frightened him so much was that whoever it was had a mask on his face and cried out 'like a rat' before running back to his room. Although Utterson tries to reassure him that these terrible changes are due to some illness, Poole is adamant that this dwarfish creature is not Dr Jekyll whom he believes has most certainly been murdered. He adds that he is convinced that the masked figure is that of Hyde, not so much because of his appearance but because of the recognisable chill its presence gave him.

See if you can you find other examples of the use of the mask ***motif***

Utterson decides to break down the door despite the pleas from within the doctor's room which are spoken not in the voice of Jekyll but clearly that of Hyde.

The dying Hyde is revealed.

When the two men break in, they find the dying Hyde, his body dressed in the doctor's clothes, which are far too big for him.

The two men begin a fruitless search for the body of Jekyll and when they return to the doctor's room they find, amongst other things, a mirror whose presence in the midst of scientific equipment is puzzling to them. Even more strange are the contents of a large envelope addressed to Utterson. Inside is a redrawn copy of the Will with the lawyer's own name replacing that of Hyde, a note from Jekyll, written that day, telling Utterson to read Lanyon's narrative which he had received earlier and, finally, a 'considerable packet' which the lawyer immediately puts in his pocket, urging Poole to keep its existence a secret.

Jekyll has changed his Will.

COMMENT

Notice the description of Poole and its similarity to other descriptions of characters in earlier chapters.

This chapter opens with the dramatic entrance of Poole. This is not the first time we have met a character whose appearance has been gravely altered by some terrible shock. He will not even look Utterson in the face. Why is this? Does this hint at something he is afraid or ashamed of? The journey of the two men to Jekyll's house takes place in a storm. They and the surrounding neighbourhood are attacked by a ferocious wind which seems to **symbolise** (see Literary Terms) Utterson's 'crushing anticipation of calamity' (p. 48).

Poole's description of the broken voice of the presence within the cabinet, whose demands for the drug grow ever more desperate, almost makes us feel a sense of pity. The servant's sighting of the masked figure, who when surprised cries out 'like a rat' (p. 52) and runs from him not only helps us to share Poole's terror but emphasises the secretive and furtive nature of whoever or whatever the creature is, as it desperately attempts to evade detection. Here the beast is out in the open. Notice how Poole describes it as moving 'like a monkey' (p. 54).

Note Stevenson's use of animal imagery

Before Poole tells us, we are convinced that this figure is Hyde, the beast himself, and perhaps share the judgement of the two men, that he has murdered Jekyll, whose body lies within the cabinet. When the door is broken down, there is 'a dismal screech as of mere animal terror' (p. 56) from inside the cabinet. There are several puzzling details, among them the oversized clothes on the body of Hyde, the mirror and 'the pious work … annotated … with blasphemies' (p. 59). How can their presence be explained there? The two men are bewildered by what they have seen and the chapter ends, as others have done, with a plea for secrecy.

Think why a mirror might be needed in a scientific laboratory.

GLOSSARY

unseemly unsuitable
lamentation weeping
knife-boy the boy who cleaned the table knives
book-learned formally educated
malefactor wrong doer

TEST YOURSELF (Section III: Chapters 6–8)

A Identify the speaker.

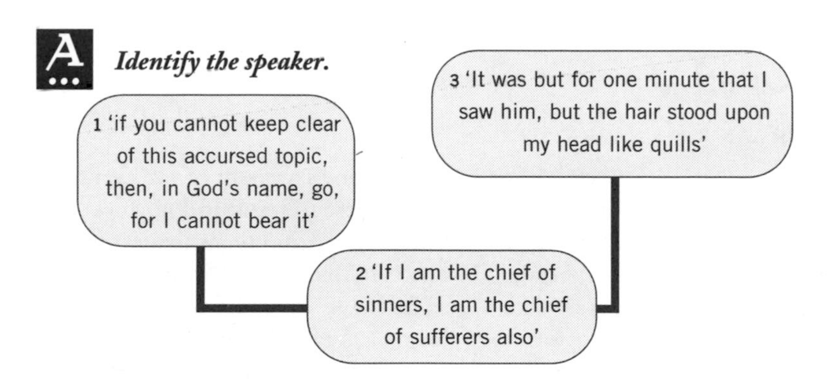

Identify the persons 'to whom' this comment refers.

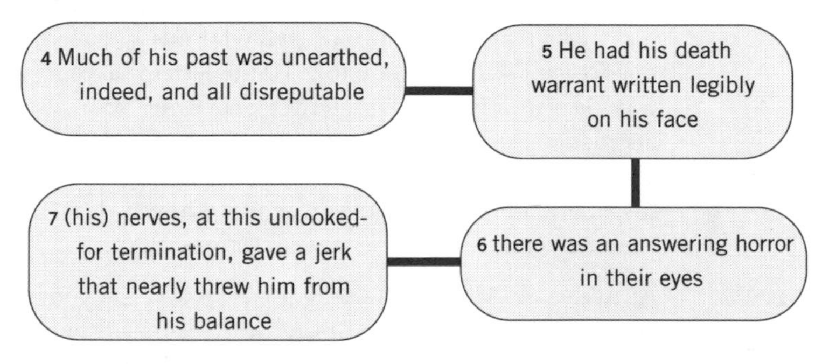

Check your answers on page 80.

Consider these issues.

a Consider what terrible crimes might Hyde have committed during his disappearance?

b Lanyon almost welcomes his own death.

c The atmosphere of secrecy which dominates the chapter.

d There is no precise description of what exactly Utterson and Enfield saw in the face of Jekyll.

e The gradual crumbling of the lawyer's inner calm.

f The mixture of fear and pity which the author makes us feel for the creature behind the door.

SECTION IV THE REVELATION

DR LANYON'S NARRATIVE

This is the first full revelation of the truth about Jekyll and Hyde.

Utterson reads his dead friend's account of the events concerning Jekyll, which were to result in Lanyon's death. The doctor had received an urgent request from Jekyll, begging him to carry out a list of instructions. He was to go to Jekyll's house where he was to enter the doctor's room in the laboratory. Here he was to find a certain drawer and, with its contents intact, bring it back to his own house. Once at home, he was to make sure that he was alone at midnight in order to admit personally a messenger from Jekyll who was to collect the drawer. The desperate tone of the letter makes it very clear to Lanyon that failure to carry out his instructions would result in the certain death or disappearance of Jekyll. Although he is deeply suspicious and fears for Jekyll's sanity, Lanyon does what he is told.

Think why the author has chosen midnight for the arrival of the strange messenger.

Note that Lanyon is given a choice.

At twelve o'clock, the messenger arrives and Lanyon describes his 'disgustful curiosity' at the sight of the man whose ludicrously outsized clothes would have provoked laughter in any other circumstance. Lanyon reveals the drawer to his visitor who by now is in a state of barely suppressed hysteria. The man mixes the powders from the drawer into a potion and challenges Lanyon to decide either to let him leave the house with the potion untouched or watch what is to follow and learn a great and valuable secret. Lanyon's curiosity causes him to choose the latter.

The transformation to Jekyll from Hyde.

His strange visitor drinks the potion and begins the painful transformation into Henry Jekyll. After this, Lanyon, his life 'shaken to its roots', is compelled to sit in the company of Jekyll as he reveals his terrible secrets, and the fact, which Lanyon dares not believe, that he is within one personality both Henry Jekyll, the respected physician, and the murderer of Sir Danvers Carew, Edward Hyde.

COMMENT

Think whether there are other hidden motives and what they are.

This chapter reveals to the reader, for the first time, the true nature of Jekyll's experiments and the real identity of Hyde. Lanyon reveals the contents of a letter from Jekyll begging for help. Think why Jekyll has chosen Lanyon for such a crucially important task when he had dismissed him earlier as 'an ignorant, blatant pedant' and spoken of how 'disappointed' he was in him (p. 27). Also, Jekyll chooses midnight for his messenger to arrive. What is the significance of this time in connection with the **theme** (see Literary Terms & Themes) of the novel?

*All these are **symbols** of secrecy.*

Once again, the recurring **motif** (see Literary Terms) of the locked door is used, reminding us of the **atmosphere** (see Literary Terms) of secrecy which pervades the novel. Notice the details of the door to Jekyll's cabinet, described as 'very strong, the lock excellent'. Indeed, it takes two skilled men two hours to open it (p. 63). Also note the ominous 'blood red liquor' found within the cabinet, with its 'highly pungent' smell (p. 63), surely hinting at dark, secretive and dangerous practices. The strange letter, and the bizarre contents of the cabinet disturb the already suspicious Lanyon, so much so that he arms himself with a revolver. We are reminded of the strained relationship between the two men in Lanyon's bitter description of Jekyll as 'flighty'.

Lanyon, in particular, is deeply affected by the presence of Hyde.

The description of the strange messenger is very important because of his effect on Lanyon, who experiences a 'marked sinking of the pulse' in his presence. He is at pains to point out that this feeling has nothing to do with the appearance of his visitor, however unsettling that may be. He later reflects that the cause of this personal disturbance lies not in any feelings of hatred but is 'much deeper in the nature of man'. Perhaps this figure has forced Lanyon to recognise and confront something within himself, something which he finds shocking and terrifying. The details of the messenger's strange clothes which are much too big for him do not provoke any amusement in Lanyon but 'a disgustful curiosity'.

Lanyon does not know the figure is Mr Hyde's.

The description of the figure also reveals some of the contradictions we have noticed in other characters. The 'great muscular activity' in his face contrasts with his 'great apparent debility of constitution', he is 'on fire with sombre excitement' (p. 65), and his manner is 'collected' yet he is very near to 'hysteria' (p. 66). By now, the reader has a clear idea of the identity of the messenger who has shown these contradictory tendencies previously, but Lanyon is in a much less privileged position, never having met him before.

Think who is taking revenge on Lanyon, Jekyll or Hyde.

What follows is clearly a challenge to Lanyon and everything he represents. Hyde obviously intends to teach the doctor, Jekyll's 'ignorant, blatant pedant', a terrible lesson. In his words he intends to 'settle' matters. He is in total command here, recognising that Lanyon's 'greed of curiosity' (p. 67) controls him. It is important to remember that Hyde gives him a clear choice and Lanyon, in his 'greed', chooses to watch Hyde as he drinks the potion. Lanyon, in fact, destroys himself. We now learn why Jekyll has chosen Lanyon to 'help' him. The dramatic and terrible transformation from Hyde to Jekyll has shaken his life 'to its roots'. Think what Lanyon has been forced to learn about himself and humanity in general.

GLOSSARY

registration by registered post
farrago a muddled, confused mixture
volatile ether a chemical used as an anaesthetic
portico an elegant doorway with columns
debility weakness
accoutrement clothing
metamorphoses changes
transcendental medicine medicine to take human beings beyond the realms of normal experience
moral turpitude depraved, wicked

TEST YOURSELF (Section IV: Chapter 9)

Identify the person 'to whom' this comment refers.

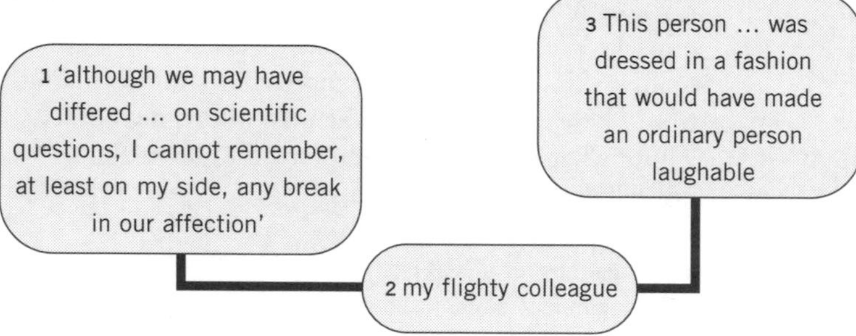

Identify the place to which this comment refers.

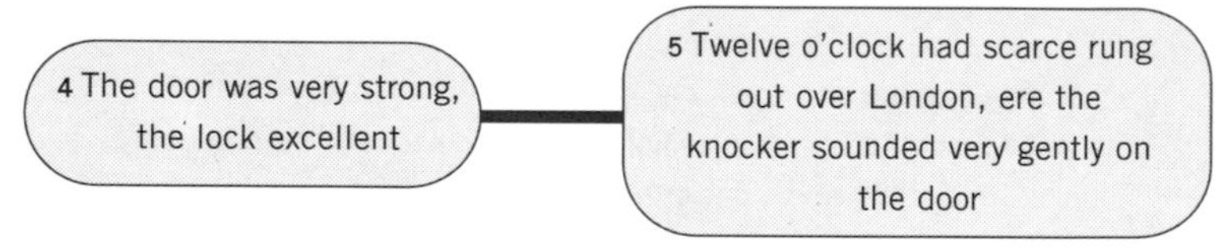

Check your answers on page 80.

Consider these issues.

a The tone of Jekyll's letter implies a bond of friendship between the two men which has been broken long ago.

b It is Lanyon's overwhelming curiosity which causes him to carry out the errand demanded of him.

c The author's description of the difficulty in breaking through the door **symbolises** (see Literary Terms) the process which the Jekyll/Hyde double will make to enter Lanyon's ordered, rational world.

d Hyde enters at midnight, the traditional hour for the worlds of the natural and supernatural to meet.

e Lanyon's curiosity controls him once again when Hyde gives him a clear choice.

f Hyde/Jekyll has deliberately chosen Lanyon to be the first and only one to witness the transformation because of his narrow views.

g Lanyon is so shocked at the secrets that Jekyll reveals to him that he cannot bring himself to write them down.

SECTION V STRUGGLE AND FALL

HENRY JEKYLL'S FULL STATEMENT OF THE CASE

Here the story of Jekyll's downfall is revealed to Utterson. He narrates how he was born into financially comfortable circumstances and progressed through his professional and social life smoothly and successfully, gaining both the respect and admiration of his contemporaries. What had long disturbed him, however, were his secret pleasures which he struggled to conceal in order to preserve his precious façade of respectability. Although he led a double life, he entered with equal enthusiasm into both the light and the dark side.

Think what 'pleasures' a respectable man like Jekyll would try hard to conceal?

Think whether Jekyll is a hypocrite.

What pained him most was that the very pleasure with which he gave himself up to his secret vices filled him with deep shame. He came to the realisation of the ultimate truth: 'that man is not truly one, but truly two', and began to experiment with the possibility of separating these two elements into two separate identities so that his 'good' side could prosper without burden of shame and his 'bad' without the restrictions of noble thoughts and ideals.

His scientific experiments led him to the discovery of a drug which could achieve this miracle. Although after he had swallowed the potion he had gone through the most terrible suffering as he was changing into Hyde, when the transformation was complete, he discovered that he felt an exhilaration in the freedom which his unrestricted evil identity now gave him. At the same time, he realised that he had shrunk in stature. Jekyll explained that this phenomenon was due to the fact that the evil side of his nature had been under strict control and therefore a lot less exercised than the good side which had gained him such respect and prosperity

Note Jekyll's elation as his evil self.

in life. However, although he was slighter and younger, the mark of evil was clearly on the face of Hyde – 'an imprint of deformity and decay'.

Jekyll also explained that the image of Hyde in the mirror did not disgust him. In fact, he found this image, his pure evil self, a great deal more natural and acceptable than his previously divided self.

The repugnance which others felt in the presence of Hyde was due to the fact that, unlike them, Hyde alone had no semblance of good; he was purely evil. Immediately he had drunk the potion he became, once again, Jekyll. However, it was not long after this that the doctor began to tire of the commendable habits of his virtuous self and yearn for the dark pleasures he could enjoy so freely as Hyde. In this light, the strange creation of the Will could now be understood as an act of self-preservation.

Hyde begins to take control.

Two months before the murder of Carew, Jekyll suffered the first terrible setback when he retired to bed in his own home as Jekyll and awoke, without the help of the potion, as Mr Hyde. The message was clearly to be seen in the increase in the size of Hyde's physical appearance: the evil side was gaining control. Jekyll had to choose between his two selves and, with some reservation, decide to give up Hyde and return to the respectable life of the doctor.

The caged beast returns with increased ferocity.

Jekyll endured this for two months before yielding to temptation and drinking the potion once again. This time, because he had been imprisoned for so long, Hyde returned more brutally and powerfully evil than before and it was this Mr Hyde who viciously and, as Jekyll explained, joyfully battered Carew to death. Although from this point Jekyll resolved to control the force of evil within him, once again, without the use of the potion, he transformed into Hyde while he was sitting in the January sunshine in a London park.

Jekyll prepares to take his life to kill Hyde.

At first, panic seized him. He could not return to his own house in search of his precious drugs and be recognised as the murderer. He realised that his salvation lay in the plan to use Lanyon which the latter had explained in his 'Narrative' to Utterson. After he had shocked his old friend, hastening his death, he returned home, but although he was close to his drugs he found that he had to increase the dosage to keep his evil identity at bay. It was clear that the identity of Jekyll was now too weak to win the struggle against Hyde and the two began to fear and despise each other. The 'statement' ends with Jekyll preparing to end his life.

COMMENT

This 'statement' not only gives us some of Jekyll's biographical details and expresses his views on the nature of the human personality but also helps to complete the reader's understanding of the **plot**.

Jekyll is from a privileged background and is very successful professionally.

He has led a double life with his public, respectable face at odds with his secret world of unspecified pleasures.

He stresses that he is no hypocrite, that he enjoys both lives equally yet is burdened by the feelings of shame which his secret life brings.

He argues that all mankind has at least two personalities.

This proves his hypocrisy because he is unable to accept his evil side as a natural part of himself.

Jekyll feels that if it were possible to separate both identities he would be able to enjoy both lives without guilt or shame.

When he changes into Hyde, he experiences elation and a sense of freedom in his increased wickedness.

He is physically smaller and younger because, up to now, the evil side of his nature had been dominated by the good and is therefore much less exercised.

The purely evil face of Hyde is welcomed by Jekyll as preferable to that of his divided personality.

Hyde soon became more dangerous and 'monstrous', growing in strength. He begins to change into Hyde without drinking the potion, proving that the evil side is taking over.

When Jekyll struggles to subdue Hyde, he cages the beast within so that when it is later released, it emerges more determined to do evil. This leads to the murder of Carew.

Hyde returns whenever Jekyll contemplates the doing of good.

The turning point for Jekyll comes when he changes into Hyde in Regent's Park. The **setting** (see Literary Terms) for this is interesting. It is a bright, clear winter's day with hints of the coming spring which will bring rebirth and renewal. This optimistic tone is shattered when Jekyll realises that he has changed into Hyde and he changes at the point when he congratulates himself for his 'active goodwill' (p. 83).

It is at this point that we realise that Jekyll is doomed.

He has only to think of good for the evil side of his nature to come back with renewed energy. There is now a terrible hatred between Jekyll's two selves and a struggle for control which Hyde is winning. As the doctor becomes weaker in his despondency, Hyde becomes stronger and more evil.

GLOSSARY

captives of Philippi an earthquake at Philippi burst open the doors of the prison where Paul and Silas were held captive, releasing them

Babylonian finger on the wall writing on the wall appearing to Daniel prophesying the end of King Belshazzar

reindue put on again

TEST YOURSELF (Section V: Chapter 10)

Identify the person 'to whom' this comment refers.

1 It was thus rather the exacting nature of my aspirations, rather than any particular degradation in my faults, that made me what I was

2 the hand which I now saw, clearly enough in the yellow light ... was lean, corded, knuckly ... and thickly shaded with a swart growth of hair

Identify the place to which this comment refers.

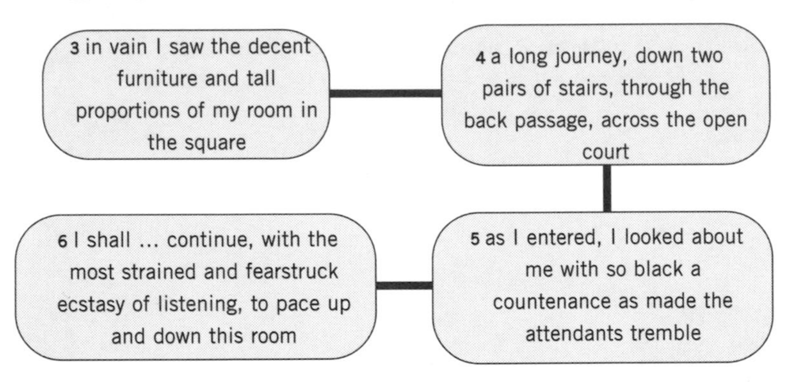

Check your answers on page 80.

Consider these issues.

a Hyde realised early in his life the essential duality or double nature of man.

b The wicked part in Jekyll appears as the lighter, younger, more sensual Hyde.

c Jekyll is not horrified, as others are, by the sight of Hyde because he accepts the wicked side of his nature.

d We are left to guess what secret pleasures Jekyll enjoyed as Hyde.

e The murder of Sir Danvers occurs because Jekyll has attempted to chain up Hyde within himself.

f Hyde would never have committed suicide. It was Jekyll who killed himself, yet even at the end Hyde again resumes control and it is his body which is found by Poole and Utterson.

COMMENTARY

THEMES

THE MEANING OF 'MR HYDE'

Dr Jekyll and Mr Hyde has been described amongst other things as a **parable** (see Literary Terms) of the struggle between good and evil, a mystery story, a classic Victorian tale of the supernatural (Stevenson himself described it as 'a fine bogey tale'), a critique of a male-dominated Victorian society, a representation of both sides of the author's personality, an expression of the father/son relationship and even a warning about the dangers of dabbling with drugs. It is a story which has exercised a considerable degree of fascination since its publication and, as can be seen above, has also provoked a variety of interpretations. One of the best ways to explore a novel in depth is to consider its **themes** (see Literary Terms). Although these are discussed for you below, don't let this stop you finding some of your own. In this way you will be contributing to a debate which has flourished for over a century.

THE DOUBLE

The divided self

The single dominant **theme** in *Dr Jekyll and Mr Hyde* is that of the double, the divided nature of man and that things are not always what they appear. Stevenson was preoccupied with this **theme** throughout his life and it appears in several of his works (see Robert Louis Stevenson's Background). It is, however, worth remembering that the author, through Jekyll, does not argue that there are only two personalities within man but that there may be many and that the evil part may only account for a small proportion.

The **theme** of the double is expressed mainly through the characters (see Characters). Obviously, Hyde represents the well-respected Jekyll's evil nature. Utterson has many subtle contradictions in his character and his friendship with his kinsman Richard Enfield seems to flourish because and not in spite of the fact that he is a man who is the complete opposite to him in many ways. Just as Jekyll is drawn to Hyde, Utterson is drawn to Enfield and vice versa. Lanyon is described as 'somewhat theatrical' (p. 18), suggesting that he is not all that he seems and the woman at Hyde's rooms 'had an evil face smoothed by hypocrisy; but her manners were excellent'.

HYPOCRISY

Hyde reveals the dark side in all of us.

In his treatment of his central **theme**, Stevenson was keen to expose the hypocrisy exhibited in all his characters and he does this largely through their reactions to Hyde (see Characters). No-one seems to be able to pinpoint what it is that is actually so repugnant about him but he provokes such extremely violent and antagonistic responses in all who encounter him. Here Stevenson is arguing that Hyde represents the dark side which is present in all people. Clearly, the characters in the novel are unable to recognise this and the abhorrence which they have for Hyde is an expression of the distaste which all human beings have for accepting this unpalatable truth. In wanting to kill Hyde, they are rejecting what is in fact part of their true selves and so are guilty of hypocrisy.

SUPPRESSION CAN LEAD TO VIOLENCE

In fact Stevenson is making a very important point which is every bit as relevant today as it was in the nineteenth century. This is that the suppression of the less socially acceptable facets of the human personality can lead to sudden, violent outpourings such as seen in

Hyde's murder of Sir Danvers Carew and in the real-life murders committed in the East End of London in 1888. The greatest hypocrite in the novel is Jekyll. Although he admits that he enjoys the wicked part of his nature, he cannot accept it as a natural part of him and therefore seeks to separate it from him in his scientific experiments. This denial leads to his destruction.

Note the symbols of duality.

Several **symbols** (see Literary Terms) are used throughout the novel to explore the **theme** of the double. One of the most powerful is the contrast between the rear and the front entrances to Dr Jekyll's house. The front door is elegant and pleasing to the eye and the hall and dining room warm, comfortable and well appointed. This is where Jekyll is seen and represents his public face. The rear door is dingy and dilapidated and leads to the gloomy interior of the old dissecting rooms which form part of Jekyll's laboratory. This obviously represents the secret, furtive and evil side of his nature. Hyde is only ever seen here, never at the front of the house.

THE BEAST IN MAN

Also part of the central **theme**, in its exploration of the different facets of the human personality, is the author's fascination with the beast in man (see Context & Setting). This is obviously represented in his creation of Hyde (see Characters) who is described throughout by others in terms of animal **imagery** (see Literary Terms).

SECRECY AND CONTROL

Stevenson uses several **symbols** (see Literary Terms) to represent the predominant **atmosphere** (see Literary Terms) of secrecy in the novel. These are in the form of locked doors, barred windows and windowless structures. The desire for secrecy is often expressed by characters in **dialogue** (see Literary Terms).

STRUCTURE

THE USE OF SEVERAL NARRATORS

Film versions have exploited popular notions of the novel.

The story of Dr Jekyll and Mr Hyde is known by many more people than those who have actually read the text. This is due to the fact that between 1920 and 1953 no less than four film versions appeared. While they endeavoured to keep the central idea intact, namely the results of Jekyll's strange laboratory experiments, they sought to make the **plot** (see Literary Terms) more palatable to contemporary audiences by altering essential details according to what they perceived as public taste. These variants were based on the final fifth of the text, 'Henry Jekyll's Full Statement of the Case' and ignore the viewpoints of the other characters, thus missing much of the depth and richness of the story.

In the novel, we are told the tale through the eyes of Enfield, Utterson, Lanyon and finally Jekyll himself and this allows us to see more clearly into their characters and relationships. Using this technique of **multiple perspectives** (see Literary Terms), Stevenson also heightens the mystery and suspense of the story.

AUTHENTICATION

One other technique adopted by Stevenson is that of **authentication** (see Literary Terms). By revealing the **plot** (see Literary Terms) through letters, diaries and, finally, a casebook, the author makes us feel that we are involved in an intimate revelation of true feelings and events rather than simply being told a story.

A PROBLEM FOR THE MODERN READER

Dr Jekyll and Mr Hyde was written as a mystery story.

Today, most people already know that Jekyll and Hyde are one and the same person before beginning to read the novel. This places the reader in a much more privileged position than his Victorian counterpart, although it certainly reduces the enjoyment. The Victorian reader may or may not have guessed the truth but it is not until the penultimate chapter, 'Dr Lanyon's Narrative', that Jekyll's terrible secret is revealed. Up to that point, we are given fascinating glimpses of Hyde through the eyes of the other characters and, as well as drawing us into the mystery of the story, these tell us important things about the characters themselves. In fact it can be said that up until the last two chapters, *Dr Jekyll and Mr Hyde* is a gripping mystery story.

CHARACTERS

Writing in *The Divided Self*, the critic Masao Miyoshi argued that 'The important men of the book … are all unmarried, intellectually barren, emotionally stifled, joyless'. Is this a fair description of the main characters in *Dr Jekyll and Mr Hyde*?

GABRIEL UTTERSON

Solid, reliable yet full of contradictions

Most of the novel is revealed through this character. We explore events with him, making the same predictions and often drawing the same erroneous conclusions. He is a man of complete integrity and although he is somewhat dour we trust him completely. He is, however, a very complex character, full of contradictions and these are expressed in the very first page of the novel. The author gives us a lengthy

description of this man, yet, at the end of it, we still do not feel as if we know him. Later in the story we recognise, perhaps more importantly, that he knows very little about himself and, perhaps, learns something fundamental from his involvement in the 'strange case' of Jekyll and Hyde.

Although a respected and obviously successful man, he is very cold. There seems to be little regard in him for company and conversation. Indeed, he is 'embarrassed in discourse' (p. 9) – surely a serious fault in a lawyer whose trade is dealing with people and their problems! Yet, this 'dreary' man is somehow lovable! Why is this? We are told that, after a glass or two of wine, 'something eminently human beaconed from his eye' (p. 9), yet this would never be reflected in his speech.

His life seems to be one long act of self-denial and secrecy (see Themes). His enjoyment of the theatre and good wine reveals a more joyful and sensual side to his nature but this has all been suppressed. Utterson reveals nothing of his inner self to the outside world. His strange friendship with Enfield, with whom he has little or nothing in common, is a source of great puzzlement to those who knew him. When they are together we are told that they 'looked singularly dull' and 'said nothing'. What does this tell us of what Utterson looks for in a 'friend'?

Throughout the story, he fails to allow the 'strange case' of Jekyll and Hyde to enter his carefully structured world. He has one view of reality and will admit no other. To him 'the fanciful was the immodest'. Therefore, when there are opportunities for new awareness, such as Enfield's revelations about the sinister Mr Hyde, he resists the challenge and, as usual, this resistance is in the form of a conspiracy of secrecy (see Themes). Like Jekyll, Utterson has a past which is not entirely blameless. Like the many contradictions in his character, this too is evidence of his 'dual nature'. When thinking back, he is 'humbled to the dust by the many ill things he had done' and thankful for 'the many that he had come so near to doing, yet avoided'. He is, however, not a judgemental man and does not condemn others.

DR HASTIE LANYON

Genial in public
Conceals a dual nature
A pedant

Lanyon is one of the three **narrators** (see Literary Terms) of the story and we meet him on two occasions only, first, when he welcomes Utterson into his house and talks about Jekyll and his ignorance of Hyde, and, secondly, when again he is visited by the lawyer after the shock of his witnessing the transformation from Hyde to Jekyll. His 'Narrative', read by Utterson after Lanyon's death, concludes his role in the story. Clearly, he suffers from similar faults to his friend Utterson in that he is narrow and conceals a dual nature. A 'hearty, healthy, dapper, red-faced gentleman' whose 'geniality … was somehow theatrical to the eye' (p. 18) gives the reader the impression that this character, however sincere his inner feelings may be, is rather too concerned about his public image and is perhaps a little superficial in his emotions. Lanyon is very much the traditional scientist in contrast with Jekyll's unorthodox, other-worldly approach. He has had scientific disagreements with his old friend and this is what causes him too sever their relationship. In fact, he is very dismissive of Jekyll, describing him as 'too fanciful'. Clearly, Jekyll has challenged Lanyon's carefully established sense of order and reason with his 'unscientific balderdash' as he has Utterson with 'the lawyer's eyesore' – the Will. Jekyll's damning indictment of him as a disappointment and more bitterly 'an ignorant, blatant pedant' shows how estranged the men are, but we feel that this judgement has a ring of truth about it.

The destruction of Lanyon

The idea of 'fanciful' ideas is as disturbing and immodest to Lanyon as it is to Utterson. Lanyon's life is 'shaken to its roots' by Jekyll's revelations. Everything he stands for and all that shapes his view of reality is shattered by this new knowledge and this subsequently kills him. He reveals that he has in the past cocooned himself from reality and that this new reality is not only unacceptable to him but causes him to welcome the release which death will bring: 'I sometimes think if we knew all, we should be more glad to get away.' We learn something of the true nature of Lanyon when he is exposed to Hyde and suffers a 'disturbance' which 'bore some resemblance to incipient rigor, and was accompanied by a marked sinking of the pulse' (p. 65). Here he is in the presence of naked evil and seems almost humbled by it. This echoes Jekyll's comment in his 'Full Statement' as he confronts the mirror image of himself as Hyde: 'It seemed natural and human. In my eyes it bore a livelier image of the spirit, it seemed more express and single, than the imperfect and divided countenance that I had been hitherto accustomed to call mine' (p. 73).

Lanyon cannot bear the truth.

It would seem that, at this point, Lanyon is also forced to confront his divided self and the rottenness of his hypocrisy in the face of something pure and unashamed. He cannot bear to think that he may have his own Mr Hyde caged within him. Clearly, the Jekyll and Hyde double had planned this act of revenge on the narrow-minded Lanyon.

EDWARD HYDE

The beast in man

Hyde clearly represents 'the beast in man' and is described in a number of animalistic **images** (see Literary Terms). When Utterson confronts him he is described as 'hissing' like a cornered snake (p. 21); Poole describes him as a 'thing' which cries out 'like a rat' (p. 52); he moves 'like a monkey' (p. 54) and screams in 'mere animal terror' (p. 56). When Jekyll awakes one morning to find that the change to Hyde has become involuntary he sees that his hand is 'thickly shaded with a swart growth of hair' (p. 77) and Jekyll describes his dual personality as 'the animal within me licking the chops of memory' (p. 82). Try to find other beastlike **images** (see Literary Terms) referring to Hyde elsewhere in the text.

Note the power of Hyde's language.

His speech is different from the other characters. He lacks their verbosity, having no time for social chit-chat. In his surprise encounter with Utterson his language is clipped. He speaks in short, staccato sentences which are in the form of unnervingly direct questions: 'How did you know me?'; 'What shall it be?'; 'Whose description?; 'Who are they?' (p. 22). Finally tiring of this conversation which had been forced upon him, he bluntly accuses Utterson of having 'lied' (p. 22). When Utterson complains that this is not fitting language (p. 22), Hyde 'snarled aloud in a savage laugh' before disappearing into the house. It is not surprising that the lawyer is left 'a picture of disquietude' (p. 23) after this whirlwind encounter. Clearly, he has met more than his match.

Look at the effect of Hyde on the other characters.

Hyde's appearance is enigmatic, seeming to change as he gains in power. Enfield describes him as giving 'a strong feeling of deformity' yet 'he is not easy to describe' (p. 15). Utterson describes him as 'pale and dwarfish' and again mentions the word 'deformity'

(p. 23). He is an extraordinary mixture of 'timidity and boldness' (p. 23) yet, as every character who encounters him argues, it is not his appearance that causes the most repugnance but an uncanny influence, what Utterson calls a mixture of 'disgust, loathing and fear' (p. 23). There are frequent references to his devil-like qualities – Enfield describes him as 'like Satan' (p. 12); and Utterson as 'having Satan's signature' upon his face (p. 23). Lanyon recognises the malign influence also and describes the expression on his face with its 'remarkable combination of great muscular activity and great apparent debility of constitution' (p. 65). There appear to be contradictory forces at work in Hyde. Think why this is. And see if you can find other examples of this.

Hyde is an enigma – note the tensions within.

What is apparent throughout the novel is that although he is described as having ' a displeasing smile' (p. 23) and a 'ghastly' face (p. 66) we are never given a detailed description of this face. You must consider whether this is a mistake or something deliberate on the part of the author. If it is deliberate, think why the author is so vague here.

DR HENRY (HARRY) JEKYLL

Inscrutable and 'slyish'

Hypocritical though appearing kindly

A respected physician and chemist, we first meet Jekyll in the third chapter 'Dr Jekyll was Quite at Ease' in which he is described as 'a large, well-made, smooth-faced man of fifty, with something of a slyish cast perhaps, but every mark of capacity and kindness' (p 26). This is typical of the author's economical style through which, using few words, he can reveal the many layers of a character's personality. Notice that the doctor is 'smooth-faced', seeming to present an inscrutable exterior and therefore an air of mystery.

The phrase 'a slyish cast' opens a crack in this polished façade through which the reader begins to see his true nature. We are reminded here of Poole's description later in the novel as he describes the Jekyll/Hyde double in the laboratory as having 'a mask upon his face' (p. 52). Also, in the chapter 'The Carew Murder Case' the 'silvery-haired old woman' at Hyde's rooms is described as having 'an evil face, smoothed by hypocrisy' (p. 32). Once again, the mask **motif** (see Literary Terms) is used by the author to underline his **theme** (see Literary Terms) of duality.

Once again we see that Jekyll is a hypocrite.

Jekyll is a wealthy man and, in his Will, leaves his entire fortune to a man whom his lawyer, Utterson, thoroughly disapproves of. His autobiography is narrated in his 'Statement' which reveals that he was born into a prosperous family, had a good education and was respected by all who knew him. Although he recognises and enjoys the evil side of his nature, Jekyll is, in fact, a hypocrite because he fails to accept it as a natural part of himself.

LANGUAGE & STYLE

The dominant **theme** (see Literary Terms & Themes) of the novel, the idea of the double, is reflected in the author's choice of language. When looking at the language of the text it is important to remember that it must be considered not in isolation but as part of the whole. The use of a range of literary devices, the creation of characters and the **dialogue** (see Literary Terms) between them and the choice of vocabulary serve to emphasise the **theme** and the underlying **moral** (see Literary Terms).

DIALOGUE

The way characters speak tells us a great deal about them. The lawyer, Utterson, is cold and reserved and, as we would expect, his language is detached, calm and measured. Very rarely does he betray any emotion, although there are times when we would expect him to. Look at the sections in the novel where Utterson is confronted by terrible revelations and events. What do you notice about his language here?

Notice how character can be revealed through speech.

Lanyon's style of speech is more florid, which is appropriate for a character who has been described as somewhat 'theatrical'. He uses **colloquialisms** (see Literary Terms), classical references and is quick to mirth and displays of temper. Enfield's talk is direct and lively. A 'well-known man about town', he is a cheerful and enthusiastic conversationalist with a natural curiosity and a liking for gossip. With his use of **colloquialisms** and occasional coarseness, he is the complete opposite of his kinsman and friend Utterson.

Like Utterson, Jekyll, too, is measured and reserved in speech because also, like the lawyer, he is a keeper of secrets. Later in the novel, when he struggles with Hyde for supremacy, his reserve breaks down and his speech becomes fragmentary and littered with oaths.

Note Hyde's singular style.

Hyde's speech is in sharp contrast to all other characters. In his encounter with Utterson (p. 22) he is direct and brutal, barking out a series of questions and accusations in short sentences. He is certainly no Enfield. Interestingly, when he speaks to Lanyon before he transforms back to Jekyll he uses the doctor's elevated style. Stevenson later regarded this as a 'gross error'.

Poole, the faithful servant, is of a different social class. He lacks the reserve of the others; he is less articulate and sophisticated and is quick to show emotion. His speech is often ungrammatical, full of clichés, slang and conventional **similes** (see Literary Terms).

Look at the richness of Stevenson's prose.

If we look at some of the descriptive prose passages in the novel we see the author employing a range of literary devices. Pages 31–2 (Utterson's journey through Soho) are particularly rewarding for examples of this and so are the descriptions of the city, usually at night or early morning in which the weather contributes powerfully to the brooding and menacing **atmosphere** (see Literary Terms). Look for examples of **metaphors** and **similes, symbolism, imagery, personification** and **irony** (see Literary Terms).

IRONY

Stevenson uses **irony** (see Literary Terms) to make profound statements about the human personality. This is, of course strongly linked with the main **theme** (see Literary Terms) of the novel and contributes to the fundamental message or **moral** (see Literary Terms) which he intends to convey. The author is very economical in his descriptions and occasionally these read almost like **epigrams** (see Literary Terms).

Note the author's critical eye.

Consider the brief descriptions of
- the police officer (p. 31)
- the old woman at Hyde's Soho rooms (p. 32)

It is worthwhile considering what statements you think Stevenson is making about these two and people in general and whether you can find any more examples of **irony** in the descriptions of other characters.

SYMBOLISM

Dr Jekyll and Mr Hyde is a very carefully constructed novel and there are many **symbols** (see Literary Terms)

*Notice how the author's use of **symbols** reinforces the **theme***

throughout the text which not only contribute powerfully to the overall sense of unease and mystery but also to the author's creation of an **atmosphere** (see Literary Terms) of secrecy and hypocrisy. The contrast between the two doors to Jekyll's house (see Themes) with the rear being virtually windowless, the several references to locked doors, barred windows and the thick, muffling fog are all examples of this. Indeed, the author uses **personification** (see Literary Terms) so that the ever-present fog is almost like a character in itself, constantly stalking the city as it battles with the wind, hides the inhabitants and muffles sound. At times it even enters the houses. This helps not only to create an **atmosphere** of gloom and misery but also links with the **themes** (see Literary Terms) of secrecy and hypocrisy (see Themes) which exists in a city where the secret vices of respectable men are hidden from the public eye.

The mask **motif** (see Literary Terms): the **image** (see Literary Terms) of the mask recurs several times throughout the novel, emphasising the **theme** of the dual personality.

See if you can find other **symbols** and **images** which closely reflect the **themes** of the novel?

Part four

Study skills

How to use quotations

One of the secrets of success in writing essays is the way you use quotations. There are five basic principles:

- Put inverted commas at the beginning and end of the quotation
- Write the quotation exactly as it appears in the original
- Do not use a quotation that repeats what you have just written
- Use the quotation so that it fits into your sentence
- Keep the quotation as short as possible

Quotations should be used to develop the line of thought in your essays.

Your comment should not duplicate what is in your quotation. For example:

> **Enfield finds it difficult to describe Hyde's appearance but feels that there is something wrong, something displeasing about it, 'He is not easy to describe. There is something wrong with his appearance; something displeasing, something downright detestable.'**

Far more effective is to write:

> **Enfield finds Hyde difficult to describe but feels that there 'was something wrong with his appearance; something displeasing, something downright detestable'.**

The most sophisticated way of using the writer's words is to embed them into your sentence:

> **Enfield finds Hyde 'not easy to describe' but he had a distinct feeling that there was 'something wrong with his appearance', the effect of which was not only 'displeasing' but 'downright detestable'.**

When you use quotations in this way, you are demonstrating the ability to use text as evidence to support your ideas - not simply including words from the original to prove you have read it.

Everyone writes differently. Work through the suggestions given here and adapt the advice to suit your own style and interests. This will improve your essay-writing skills and allow your personal voice to emerge.

The following points indicate in ascending order the skills of essay writing:

- Picking out one or two facts about the story and adding the odd detail
- Writing about the text by retelling the story
- Retelling the story and adding a quotation here and there
- Organising an answer which explains what is happening in the text and giving quotations to support what you write

....

- Writing in such a way as to show that you have thought about the intentions of the writer of the text and that you understand the techniques used
- Writing at some length, giving your viewpoint on the text and commenting by picking out details to support your views
- Looking at the text as a work of art, demonstrating clear critical judgement and explaining to the reader of your essay how the enjoyment of the text is assisted by literary devices, linguistic effects and psychological insights; showing how the text relates to the time when it was written

The dotted line above represents the division between lower- and higher-level grades. Higher-level performance begins when you start to consider your response as a reader of the text. The highest level is reached when you offer an enthusiastic personal response and show how this piece of literature is a product of its time.

Coursework essay

Set aside an hour or so at the start of your work to plan what you have to do.

- List all the points you feel are needed to cover the task. Collect page references of information and quotations that will support what you have to say. A helpful tool is the highlighter pen: this saves painstaking copying and enables you to target precisely what you want to use.
- Focus on what you consider to be the main points of the essay. Try to sum up your argument in a single sentence, which could be the closing sentence of your essay. Depending on the essay title, it could be a statement about a character: Stevenson intended the reader to recognise that the evil Hyde was as natural a part of his personality as the good side and that he destroyed himself by refusing to accept this and trying to separate the two; an opinion about setting: Stevenson's nocturnal, foggy, lamp-lit city is fitting for a society where secrecy and hypocrisy dominate; or a judgement on a theme: The main theme appears to be that all human beings have at least two facets of their personality, good and evil, and that these exist in different measure.
- Make a short essay plan. Use the first paragraph to introduce the argument you wish to make. In the following paragraphs develop this argument with details, examples and other possible points of view. Sum up your argument in the last paragraph. Check you have answered the question.
- Write the essay, remembering all the time the central point you are making.
- On completion, go back over what you have written to eliminate careless errors and improve expression. Read it aloud to yourself, or, if you are feeling more confident, to a relative or friend.

If you can, try to type your essay using a word processor. This will allow you to correct and improve your writing without spoiling its appearance.

Examination essay

The essay written in an examination often carries more marks than the coursework essay even though it is written under considerable time pressure.

In the revision period build up notes on various aspects of the text you are using. Fortunately, in acquiring this set of York Notes on *Dr Jekyll and Mr Hyde*, you have made a prudent beginning! York Notes are set out to give you vital information and help you to construct your personal overview of the text.

Make notes with appropriate quotations about the key issues of the set text. Go into the examination knowing your text and having a clear set of opinions about it.

In most English Literature examinations, you can take in copies of your set books. This is an enormous advantage although it may lull you into a false sense of security. Beware! There is simply not enough time in an examination to read the book from scratch.

In the examination

- Read the question paper carefully and remind yourself what you have to do.
- Look at the questions on your set texts to select the one that most interests you and mentally work out the points you wish to stress.
- Remind yourself of the time available and how you are going to use it.
- Briefly map out a short plan in note form that will keep your writing on track and illustrate the key argument you want to make.
- Then set about writing it.
- When you have finished, check through to eliminate errors.

To summarise, these are keys to success

- **Know the text**
- **Have a clear understanding of and opinions on the storyline, characters, setting, themes and writer's concerns**
- **Select the right material**
- **Plan and write a clear response, continually bearing the question in mind**

SAMPLE ESSAY PLAN

A typical essay question on *Dr Jekyll and Mr Hyde* is followed by a sample essay plan in note form. This does not present the only answer to the question, merely one answer. Do not be afraid to include your own ideas. Remember that quotations are essential to prove and illustrate the points you make.

The first eight chapters of the novel read as a mystery story. How does Stevenson create an atmosphere of mystery and suspense, yet at the same time leave us a number of clues which help us to discover the identity of Hyde before the last two chapters?

Introduction

As well as making a profound statement about the nature of the human personality, Stevenson intended to create a gripping story which keeps the reader in suspense until the final chapters. He does this in a number of ways.

Part 1 The mystery begins

We meet Utterson, a tolerant, intelligent man who is reliable and trustworthy and never quick to judge others. He will be our guide throughout the first eight chapters and we identify with him and share in his discoveries and misconceptions.

The strange door becomes a symbol of mystery. We don't know where it leads.

We first hear of Hyde. He is difficult to describe but has a powerful effect on all who meet him and all are unable to account for these strong, unpleasant feelings. His behaviour is puzzling. He tramples on the girl not out of any act of anger but appears perfectly calm. He readily accepts his guilt and agrees to compensation.

The crowd are driven to a murderous rage by this. Enfield is as shocked by this as he is by his own and the doctor's reactions which seem completely out of character.

Hyde produces the cheque with an unmentionable name signed upon it.

Part 2
The search for Hyde – the mystery deepens

We hear of the Will and the fact that Dr Jekyll has left his entire fortune to the brute Hyde. It is because we trust Utterson that we share his concerns for his friend and as his worries increase, so do ours.

Utterson, normally a rational man, has a nightmare which is full of evil foreboding. This makes us fear the worst and deepens our desire to identify the faceless Hyde.

Utterson sees Hyde's face and hears him speak and his mixture of timidity and boldness intrigues us.

Normally so slow to judge, Utterson is struck by the feelings of profound loathing which this strange man inspires in him.

With Utterson, we begin to suspect Hyde of various crimes, including blackmail and forgery and wonder if this is why he has some hold over Jekyll. This may be so, but why is Jekyll so defensive about him and tolerant of his violence and cruelty?

We fear, like Utterson, that if Hyde knew the contents of Jekyll's Will, he would murder the doctor.

Lanyon reveals his distaste for Jekyll's unscientific experiments but does not elaborate on their nature while Jekyll strongly criticises Lanyon's narrow, traditional views. We begin to wonder what could cause such a rift between two such old and trusted friends and colleagues.

A year has passed since the last chapter. The reader wonders what unspeakable crimes Hyde has committed in that time. When he murders Carew it is clear that his capacity for evil is increasing. We fear for Jekyll's safety.

Hyde vanishes completely after the attack. He leaves evidence of ownership of several thousand pounds. How can he have gained this if not by blackmail? But also, how can such a distinctive man disappear without trace?

Part 3
The realisation

Jekyll's changed appearance and earnest promise to Utterson that he has finished with Hyde are not altogether convincing. It is at this point that our trust in the reliability of Utterson as our guide begins to break down. Perhaps he is too close to his friend Jekyll to notice the 'slyish cast' (p. 26).

The letter produced by Jekyll and supposedly written by Hyde is proved by Utterson's head clerk, Guest, to have been forged by Jekyll. Utterson is amazed at this but we begin to wonder about Jekyll's trustworthiness. Is he a liar and a forger?

Lanyon is destroyed by some terrible shock and this is obviously to do with Jekyll. What can have happened? We remember the effect that Hyde has on those who meet him. Has Jekyll introduced Lanyon to his friend? Why and how would he do this?

Enfield confirms what we suspect, that the strange door through which Hyde passes is the rear entrance to Jekyll's house and laboratory.

Jekyll suddenly withdraws from the window, significantly at the back of the house, with a look of dreadful anguish upon his face which frightens his two visitors. We feel that Jekyll is trying to resist some powerful force.

We become impatient with Utterson because he takes so long to accept the seriousness of Poole's words.

Poole's account of Jekyll's disappearance, the changed voice, the strange cries and persistent weeping, the desperate search for the drug, the strange figure in the mask and the dwarfish figure whom he is convinced is Hyde forces us to conclude that the relationship between himself and Jekyll is closer than Utterson realises and is somehow bound up with the doctor's strange unscientific experiments.

When the two men break into the doctor's cabinet and find the body of Hyde dressed in Jekyll's clothes, which are 'far too large for him', we realise the truth.

This is confirmed by the contents of the cabinet, particularly the mirror, the absence of Jekyll and the change in his Will which has not been destroyed and the written evidence that Jekyll had been there that day.

Conclusion It is impossible for the modern reader to read this novel as an unsuspecting Victorian would have done, because today Jekyll's double identity is so well known. It is, however, easy to see that Stevenson intended to keep his readers in the dark for as long as possible, while challenging them to discover the truth for themselves, by leaving a series of vital clues. The reader only begins to realise the full truth when Utterson as our guide has been dispensed with. Up to this point he has been used not only as a narrator but as a means of deepening the mystery within the story and therefore heightening the tension and suspense.

FURTHER QUESTIONS

1. Discuss Stevenson's portrayal of the nature of 'good' and 'evil' and the dual nature of man's personality in the novel, choosing two characters as your focus.
2. Throughout the novel, Hyde has a powerful effect on all who encounter him. Choose two different characters and compare how they react to Hyde, explaining any differences and/or similarities.
3. Show how Stevenson, through the themes, language and setting, creates a world of double standards and hypocrisy.
4. What is Stevenson saying about the type of men represented by the characters in the novel and the nature of the society they live in?
5. The author not only wrote this novel to present his views on the human personality but also because he wanted to shock contemporary readers out of their complacency. Show how parts of *Jekyll and Hyde* read as a horror story.
6. Jekyll is in control of Hyde at the beginning of the novel but this situation is reversed at the end. Show how this process develops throughout the first eight chapters.
7. If Hyde had written the 'Full Statement' instead of Jekyll, how would the account have been different?
8. Lanyon was the architect of his own doom. Show how he brought about his own death and how this links with the demise of Jekyll.
9. Write an imaginary dialogue, contrasting the views of Lanyon and Jekyll on the human personality, the nature of evil and the role of scientific medicine.
10. There are several narrators in Jekyll and Hyde. Discuss what each of them contributes to the novel and what their narratives reveal about them as characters.

11 Utterson, with his lack of prejudice and honest, reliable nature, is our main guide throughout the novel. In a character study of Utterson, describe his relationship with the other characters and, in examining the false conclusions he comes to, explain why he makes so many mistakes.

12 Discuss the view that *Dr Jekyll and Mr Hyde* is a parable about the nature of good and evil.

13 Imagine that Utterson has to give an account of events which took place during 'The Last Night' to Inspector Newcomen of Scotland Yard, having previously read 'Lanyon's Narrative' and 'Jekyll's Full Statement'. What would he choose to reveal and what would he conceal?

14 Consider the language Stevenson uses in the novel and how it underpins his themes of the double personality, secrecy, hypocrisy and the 'beast in man'. You should refer to his use of dialogue, imagery and irony.

Part five

Cultural connections

Broader perspectives

The history of the 'horror story'

The 'horror story' reached its fullest expression in the great works of the nineteenth century, particularly in the **Victorian age** (see Literary Terms). Although a number of these works will only be known to literary historians or enthusiasts of the genre, perhaps three have become an established part of our culture and have been used and interpreted with varying degrees of merit. These are Mary Shelley's *Frankenstein* (1818), Bram Stoker's *Dracula* (1897) and Stevenson's *Dr Jekyll and Mr Hyde* (1886).

The genesis of horror

The development of these stories can be traced back to the so-called 'Gothic Novels', which came about largely as a reaction to the stress which the eighteenth century had placed on the supreme value of reason and the values that go with reason. This emphasis was considered to stifle emotional expression and, in particular, deny the darker and more mysterious forces of the personality which were thought of as uncivilised, and therefore medieval and Gothic.

The term Gothic then became associated with the mysterious, the fantastic and, occasionally, the horrific, appealing to the emotional side of human experience and throwing off the shackles of reason. The first Gothic novel was Horace Walpole's *Castle of Otranto* (1764), set in Italy during the Middle Ages. Other notable examples were M.G. Lewis's *The Monk* (1796) and Mrs Ann Radcliffe's *The Mysteries of Udolpho* which became famous as the object of **satirical** (see Literary Terms) treatment by Jane Austen in *Northanger Abbey*. These novels shared a similar **setting** (see Literary Terms), namely the Europe of the Middle Ages, but soon the term Gothic began to apply to any literature dealing with the fantastic and mysterious, irrespective of period or **setting**. Thus William Beckford's *Vathek* (1796), was set in ninth-century Arabia and Shelley's *Frankenstein* in contemporary Switzerland and the polar region. However, it was in the first half of the nineteenth century that stories of the supernatural, as we know them today, established themselves as a distinct literary form. Although as in Gothic fiction there was an implicit warning against a reliance on simple rational explanation, the Victorian ghost story broke away from the Gothic tradition of the use of remote backgrounds and times to the employment of domestic and contemporary **settings**. Perhaps the earliest example of this is Elizabeth Gaskell's *The Old Nurse's Story* which dates from 1852.

The development of the realistic ghost story

Instead of improbable people and events taking place in impossible places we began to see ordinary human beings in familiar environments. Therefore, when an agent of the supernatural entered such an immediately recognisable world, the reader would become all the more inclined to believe the unbelievable. It was easier to sympathise with the characters and to feel their fears. In other words, the shudder experienced in the reading of such stories was caused by the belief, however temporary, that such dreadful events could actually happen to us.

Other important examples of the genre include several of the stories of J.S. Le Fanu including 'Green Tea' (1869) and 'Madam Crowl's Ghost' (1870); Charles Dickens's 'The Signalman' (1866); Stevenson's own 'The Body Snatcher' (1884) and Henry James's 'The Romance of Certain Old Clothes' (1868). The **Victorian age** (see Literary Terms) saw major developments in scientific knowledge and a resulting secularism and materialism which seemed to frown upon the irrational. However, just in case man felt that he was safe from supernatural intervention and judgement, the ghost story told readers that crimes would never go unpunished. Captain Barton, a character in Le Fanu's 'The Watcher' (1851) expresses his and most probably the writer's belief:

> There does exist beyond this a spiritual world – a system whose workings are generally, in mercy, hidden from us – a system which may be, and which is sometimes, partially and terribly revealed. I am sure – I know … that there is a God – a dreadful God – and that retribution follows guilt, in ways the most mysterious and stupendous – by agencies the most inexplicable and terrible.

The vengeful ghost

It was in the late part of the nineteenth century that the ghost story began to be more heavily imbued with a flavour of horror, in which an overreaching curiosity or an unpunished crime was resolved by the intervention of the returning dead, often in the most tangible form, whose twin motives were always revenge and destruction. These agencies were not necessarily avenging angels, acting out of any sense of justice and morality but often beings who exhibited a thirst for evil. The best examples of stories of this kind can be found in the collections of M.R. James, such as *Ghost Stories of an Antiquary* (1904).

Although not a ghost story as such, *Dr Jekyll and Mr Hyde* is rooted in the Victorian tradition. The clear intention is to make the reader experience fear, the settings are contemporary and recognisable and the spirit, if that is how Hyde can be described, is clearly vengeful and evil. Also, Jekyll clearly goes too far in his research, seeking in a contemporary phrase 'to play God'. However, Stevenson's novel is obviously more than that, in that it shares with the Gothic story a desire to explore the hidden forces within the human personality as well as offering a critique of the strict repressions of the Victorian moral code.

FILM VERSIONS

Four film versions have been made of *Dr Jekyll and Mr Hyde*, but none adequately conveys the depth and richness of Stevenson's novel, because they omit the different viewpoints and concentrate on only a small section of the novel (see Structure).